The Psychology and Economics of Happiness

Much attention has been given to the economics of everyday life, which typically applies economic principles to the analysis of the different choices that people face under different situations. Yet there are hardly any books on the economics of life – an economics that takes the finite lifespan as the starting point and that looks at how one can maximise the subjective value from life given the constraint of the limited lifespan.

In this volume, Lok Sang Ho suggests that the lack of progress in happiness among developed countries despite significant economic growth is due to a deficit of 'mental goods', rather than a lack of material goods. The author stresses the role of culture and mental habits in determining the efficacy of gaining mental goods, which includes love, a sense of security and autonomy, contentment, self-esteem, self-acceptance and freedom from anxiety. Drawing on empirical research, the book explores how to invest, work and consume from a whole-life perspective, arguing that every action – consumption, investment or work – should enhance the total quality of life. This overriding concern about life itself is known as love.

The Psychology and Economics of Happiness uses the analytical framework of economists on a subject studied by positive psychologists, drawing both from empirical evidence and from psychological literature. It will be of interest to researchers and academics interested in economic and positive psychology, as well as those from related fields keen to learn more about living fuller, happier lives.

Lok Sang Ho is Professor and Head of the Department of Economics and Director of the Centre for Public Policy Studies at Lingnan University, Hong Kong.

'The *Psychology and Economics of Happiness* is a rare gem! Drawing on scientific research findings from economics and positive psychology it shows how we can maximize our positive life experiences within the constraints of a limited lifespan. Taking a whole life perspective, Professor Lok Sang Ho gives very coherent guidance on how to live so as to maximize satisfaction in terms of acquiring physical goods and mental goods including a sense of achievement, autonomy, dignity, and self-acceptance. This is a book that everybody should read.'

Professor Alan Carr, School of Psychology, University College Dublin, Ireland

'After reading this volume it is easy to see why it is crucial to have a book that focuses solely on the economics of love, life and happiness. This is because economics, especially behavioral economics, opens to us a whole new and highly useful way of understanding these crucial and pivotal topics [. . .] Professor Ho brings us a much needed, timely addition to this vastly important, worthy endeavor.'

Dr J. Richard Cookerly, Clinical Fellow of the American Association for Marital and Family Therapy

The Psychology and Economics of Happiness

Love, life and positive living

Lok Sang Ho

LONDON AND NEW YORK

First published 2014
by Routledge
27 Church Road, Hove, East Sussex, BN3 2FA

and by Routledge
711 Third Avenue, New York, NY 10017

Routledge is an imprint of the Taylor & Francis Group, an informa business

© 2014 L. S. Ho

The right of L. S. Ho to be identified as author of this work has been asserted by him in accordance with sections 77 and 78 of the Copyright, Designs and Patents Act 1988.

All rights reserved. No part of this book may be reprinted or reproduced or utilised in any form or by any electronic, mechanical, or other means, now known or hereafter invented, including photocopying and recording, or in any information storage or retrieval system, without permission in writing from the publishers.

Trademark notice: Product or corporate names may be trademarks or registered trademarks, and are used only for identification and explanation without intent to infringe.

British Library Cataloguing in Publication Data
A catalogue record for this book is available from the British Library

Library of Congress Cataloging in Publication Data
Ho, Lok-sang.
  The psychology and economics of happiness: love, life and positive living/Lok Sang Ho.
  pages cm
  Includes bibliographical references.
  1. Economics—Sociological aspects. 2. Happiness—Economic aspects. 3. Quality of life—Economic aspects. I. Title.
  HM548.H62 2014
  306—dc23
  2013024492

ISBN: 978-0-415-70616-2 (hbk)
ISBN: 978-1-315-88746-3 (ebk)

Typeset in Galliard
by Swales & Willis Ltd, Exeter, Devon

Printed and bound in Great Britain by
TJ International Ltd, Padstow, Cornwall

Contents

List of figures vii
List of tables viii
Foreword 1: J. Richard Cookerly ix
Foreword 2: Yew-Kwang Ng xii
Preface xiv
Acknowledgements xviii

1 Introduction to the economics of life 1

2 Love and the economics of love 11

3 The role of culture in household production 23

4 Mental capital and habit formation, with a digression to spiritual capital 32

5 The happiness formula 40

6 Marriage, mental capital and happiness 56

7 More on mental goods: self-actualisation versus vanity 62

8 Insight 65

9 Fortitude 73

10 Engagement: living with a purpose 81

11 Three happinesses and transcendental happiness 88

12 Avoiding regrets and coming to terms with past errors 94

13 Avoiding worries and coming to terms with an uncertain future and negative emotions 99

14 The paradox of choice: more choices and more sophisticated products need not translate into greater happiness　105

15 The holistic perspective on life, successful living and happiness　110

16 Epilogue　118

References　122
Index　127

Figures

1.1	Seeing the big picture to truly optimise	3
1.2	Household production	6
3.1	Efficient household production	29
3.2	Inefficient household production	29
4.1	Mental capital	33
4.2	Spiritual capital	33
5.1	Wellbeing (WB) – age profile in the United States	53
11.1	Hong Kong's Happiness Index 2005–2011	91
13.1	'Blessed'	101
14.1	Results of an online marriage happiness poll	107

Tables

5.1	LIFE scores by sex and age groupings: telephone survey data from Hong Kong	48
5.2	Regression results using 2008–2012 telephone survey pooled data (with yearly dummies) from Hong Kong	49
5.3	Regression results using online survey (2011) data from Hong Kong	50
5.4	Baseline regression on World Value Survey wave 4 data (2005)	51
5.5	World Value Survey results (wave 4) with effects of demographic variables and other variables added	51
5.6	World Value Survey results (wave 4) with country variables included and year dummies added (2005–2008)	52
5.7	Appendix: LIFE score definitions based on World Value Survey wave 4 data	55
6.1	LIFE scores between single and married by age (online survey 2011)	57
6.2	LIFE scores in Hong Kong by sex, age and marital status 2011, online data	57
6.3	Gender and marriage status effects on happiness/discounts (online survey)	58
6.4	Gender and marriage status effects on happiness/discounts (telephone surveys)	59
6.5	Appendix: Online survey 2011 full model results	61
11.1	Three happinesses over the life cycle 2008	91
11.2	Regression results on happiness versus life satisfaction using 2011 telephone survey from Hong Kong	92

Foreword I

Intrigued, with a touch of anticipation and, I confess, with a bit of scepticism I started reading Professor Ho's manuscript for this book. Questions arose within me. How would the average reader benefit from this volume? What does economics have to offer that psychology and relational research have not already discovered? What might an economic approach bring to the understanding of love, life and happiness? These were subjects dear to both my personal and professional endeavours as a relational psychotherapist who for decades has laboured with troubled couples, dysfunctional families and lonely individuals searching for healthy, real love. Could people like me counsel with profit from reading this book? What useful insights and knowledge might a professor of economics add to those of us whose professional life has been spent studying these topics? As I began reading, it immediately became clear that Dr Ho and his book had an abundance of highly useful things to offer everyone.

This book's excellence lies in bringing together a delightful interweave of western scientific and eastern artful treatments of its subject matter. Moving poetry combines with illuminating facts and figures, complete with charts, to charm and enlighten the reader. Examples from both oriental and occidental cultures blend with ancient and modern mind sets. All these are well used in this volume to enrich us with usable knowledge and to stimulate creative cognition for understanding love, happiness and life itself.

In recent years, scientists in many fields began to conduct rigorous research into the positive aspects of love and happiness, and how life can be lived well. Thanks to Professor Ho's fine contributions in this volume, the field of behavioural economics can be seen to add much to this growing bounty. His many conceptualisations and his factual information are presented in very human and humane terms. This book is filled with clear, potent examples, gentle care and intelligent descriptions – all of which makes for a very fine read.

In this volume I discovered, as I think you will, many new, refreshing formulations and schemas for comprehending the dynamics of love, life and happiness. I was introduced to novel conceptualisations accompanied by vivid, and sometimes new, terms like 'mental goods', 'mental capital', 'social capital', 'happiness set range', 'choice paradox', 'sunk costs' and a good many others. All of these began creatively enriching and expanding my thinking on the important topics being addressed.

Right from the first chapter, Professor Ho shows us how to understand better and deal with life better through the insights of a modern, behavioural, economics-based approach. This quite quickly is evident in his economics-grounded presentations concerning maximising the desirable in love and life. Dr Ho addresses the pertinent questions dealing with why we do well to view love, happiness and life through the lens of an economics-informed thought process. He presents a number of intriguing, new and somewhat controversial points like how 'household production' yields a more savvy comprehension than do the terms consumer or consumption. His argument for how mental goods and mental capital have greater significance than tangible goods and wealth is presented in a most engaging style.

I particularly was captivated by Professor Ho's treatment of love. Of course, that might be because healthy, real love is my particular area of research and practitioner interest. Dr Ho, ever so rightly in my opinion, points out how the new economics of love is about value and not mere consumer acquirement, as older, mainstream dreary economics might suggest. Ho's writing on the importance of distinguishing between 'romantic affinity' and real love was something I can and will cite to many people. His chapter on marriage and happiness discloses valuable ideas about who may be made more happy and who more unhappy via marriage. This supports, ever so well, a key concept of Professor Ho's that has to do with the immense importance of 'mental capital' to successful, happy marriage.

Repeatedly cited in this wonderful book are the revealing results of a massive, large-scale, long-range, research endeavour. This research delves into a host of variables having to do with happiness itself being conducted at Dr Ho's university and in conjunction with his work. Professor Ho reports some of the highly important findings flowing from his own Hong Kong Lingnan University and its Centre for Public Policy Studies happiness surveys. Once you have read what Ho reports here, let me suggest to more serious students that an indepth review of these empirical findings is likely to be most valuable. I also recommend reviewing this research to anyone and everyone interested in really looking into the dynamics of happiness.

Dr Ho frequently waxes wonderfully poetic and scientifically erudite in his treatment of culture's effects on love, life and happiness. He includes a broad range of topic areas to consider like environmental impact, the unethical tendencies and corrupt practices of more and less advantaged people, the levelling off of 'emotional wellbeing' after reaching a certain financial level, and the importance of 'spiritual capital' to successful living. Strongly emphasised are the likely consequences of wisely investing our mental capital and how that can dramatically increase our love and happiness returns. How 'negative mental capital' and 'sunk cost bygones' can sabotage our lives is succinctly, clearly and forcefully dealt with in earnest. The discussions concerning insight live up to their promise by providing many refreshing insights into old topics like the 'seven deadly sins' and the eastern *Butterfly Lovers* tragedies, along with western tales of unrequited love and its travails. The wonders of the *Song of the Truthful Mind*, 'the three happinesses' hypothesis and the marvels of transcendental happiness are likely to draw you in and help you explore deeper into this fine 'economic' work. But beware. It also is likely to draw you into exploring your own, inner, mysterious being in ways you might not expect.

Highly informative sections of this book give tools and tenets for avoiding the constraints of obsessive regret and for achieving the positive handling of 'true errors' of the past. Also presented are ways to diminish worry and useless obsessions. The practical use of mindfulness for coming to terms with various negative-capital states is brought to light. These are but a few of the many gems that saturate Professor Ho's book.

An economics of life approach leads Professor Ho to an artfully presented formula for enduring happiness in life. His formula can be used to build a broad understanding of one's own life position, help in life redirection and provide powerful assistance in turning life negatives into positives. How to arm yourself with 'key criteria' for wise decision-making and avoid 'distractions' from good decision making also are among the numerous eye openers included in this volume.

In presenting all these superb thought tools and life-enriching approaches one comes to see Professor Ho as a true pioneer in the awakening application of behavioural economics to the wider, higher and deeper aspects of our existence. After decades of learning and practising in the health and behavioural sciences it came as a distinct delight to have Dr Ho's 'economics' endow me with wonderful, additional ways to understand human behaviour related to love, happiness and life itself.

After reading this volume it is easy to see why it is crucial to have a book that focuses solely on the economics of love, life and happiness. This is because economics, especially behavioural economics, opens to us a whole new and highly useful way of understanding these crucial and pivotal topics. We live in a time that thirsts for everything we can do to bring more health, real love and true happiness to life. Professor Ho brings us a much-needed, timely addition to this vastly important, worthy endeavour.

I utterly devoured this book and I suspect you will too!

Dr J. Richard Cookerly
Clinical Fellow of the American Association
for Marital and Family Therapy

Foreword 2

It is a pleasure and honour to write a foreword for Professor Lok Sang Ho's very useful book, *The Psychology and Economics of Happiness: Love, life and positive living*.

I have known Lok Sang for three decades and got to know him well since my visit to the Chinese University of Hong Kong in 1997. He strikes me as not only a very competent economist but also as someone with passions for social improvements, especially in public policy. He belongs to a small proportion of economists for not being too narrowly focused on purely economics-related issues, but having a wider perspective. Being a prolific writer in both English and Chinese, in both scholarly and popular outlets, he has made important contributions not only in his main area of public policy, but also in macroeconomics, international finance, labour economics, urban economics and environmental economics. His contributions cover both general conceptual and policy issues and specific local (especially Hong Kong and mainland China) and global economy issues. In fact, his contributions and interests go beyond economics, including on the very specialised and demanding (including the command of ancient Chinese) interpretation and translation of the *Daodejing*, which is attributed to Chinese philosopher Laozi.

Lok Sang has made significant contributions in happiness studies, including several books, on happiness indices in Hong Kong, and on the importance of LIFE (Love, Insight, Fortitude and Engagement). We are fortunate to have such a well-qualified scholar with a wide perspective to write a very useful book on a most important topic. Numerous exchanges with Lok Sang have convinced me that he shares with me the view that happiness is the ultimate objective for individuals and the society they constitute. I may be a little more thorough (though others may regard it as more narrow or shallow) than many others in believing that, provided that we include relevant effects on others (not confined only to humans) and in the future, happiness is, or at least should be, the only thing that is of ultimate value. Lok Sang and I argued several times on this and related issues. Each time, we ultimately agreed that there are really no differences, at least no fundamental differences, between us, though at least some differences in emphasis and ways of presentation linger. Perhaps even some fundamental differences may still exist, as on the Kantian 'categorical imperative' discussed below.

This book is very well written with excellent English, despite the fact that the author's mother tongue is not English. It is very readable and most readers should have no difficulties in understanding the messages. Most readers, and younger people in particular, will benefit a lot from reading it. It is most suitable for general readers. While there are books on similar topics separately, the blending of economics, love, life and happiness and combining western and eastern wisdom is unique.

While I agree with most parts of this book, I do have some reservations on a few aspects. For one example, in Chapter 5, it is stated: 'Ageing is seen to have a negative effect on happiness, after the LIFE variables have been controlled'. This may be valid in a technical or statistical sense but could be misleading to unwatchful readers. I suspect that, up to a fairly high age, ageing increases happiness largely through increasing LIFE (as this book demonstrates). If we hold LIFE constant or take off the LIFE-enhancing effects of ageing, then ageing could decrease happiness through other effects. Instead of saying that ageing has a negative effect on happiness after LIFE variables have been controlled, I would rather say that ageing probably increases happiness, at least partly through increasing LIFE.

As another example, in Chapter 10 on engagement, Lok Sang quotes Kant approvingly and seems to regard the realisation of one's full potential as a 'categorical imperative' that one should pursue. I strongly disagree with Kantian moral philosophy and believe that no categorical imperative (including the realisation of full potential) should be pursued without regard to the effects on happiness for all. Though the advice to realise one's full potential may be desirable in 99 out of 100 cases, it is bad moral philosophy not to give due consideration to the ultimate value of happiness. I have argued elsewhere (including in a forthcoming book on happiness in Chinese to be published by Fudan University Press in the middle of 2013) that the 'categorical imperative' in ancient China that 'a woman should not marry twice' has caused huge suffering and the current 'categorical imperative' that 'life is sacrosanct' (thus condemning euthanasia categorically) is causing probably even greater suffering.

The fact that I disagree with significant aspects of this book and yet strongly recommend it should convince thoughtful readers even more of its worthiness. Get it and read it before you forget to the detriment of your own happiness!

Yew-Kwang Ng
Division of Economics,
Nanyang Technological University
Singapore

Preface

In recent years, there has been an increasing interest among economists in psychology and particularly in happiness studies. The works of Angus Deaton, Richard Easterlin, Bruno Frey, James Heckman, John Helliwell, Alan Krueger, Lord Richard Layard, Yew-kwang Ng and Andrew Oswald, among others, are well known. Quite a number of their works have appeared in the psychological and science journals. Oswald and Wu (2010) reported, in *Science*, one of the top journals in science, objective confirmation of subjective measures of wellbeing. In a sample of one million Americans across 50 states, the authors found a close match between people's subjective life satisfaction scores and objectively estimated quality of life. Reflecting on the validity of such subjective measures, quite a number of the works of psychologists on life satisfaction or happiness have found their way into the mainstream economics journals. Indeed, Daniel Kahneman, a psychologist, has won the Nobel Prize in Economic Science for his contribution in illuminating human behaviour.

The methodology used by economists typically interprets human behaviour as intending to maximise 'utility', which used to be regarded as synonymous with satisfaction and subjective wellbeing. Thanks to the work of behaviour economists and others like Kahneman, it is now increasingly recognised that people only maximise 'decision utility', which is a measure of how alternative choices are evaluated at the time of decision making, and that may not necessarily relate to the final utility achieved. This in part reflects the cost of information, and in part reflects flaws in human perception and uncertainty. The purpose of this book, however, is not so much to explain people's behaviour as to shed light on how subjective wellbeing can be enhanced through wiser choices and better decision making. Its starting point is the perspective that, despite information cost and flaws in perception, 'constrained maximisation' still makes sense. Constrained maximisation is also called 'the economic problem': human beings face constraints and they are supposed to do the best to maximise their wellbeing under the circumstances. Its motivation is the observation that in practice most people fail to make the most out of the opportunities that they have, and that a change in attitude, and an increase in understanding, can make a huge difference. Positive psychology is not unrealistic optimism based on faith that somehow things will work out. Positive psychology is about the will – the determination – to make the best out of every situation. Conceptually, this is really no different from 'constrained maximisation', the key concept that economists talk about!

In a typical introduction to an economics course, students are told that (micro) economics deals with *what* to produce, *how* to produce and *for whom* to produce. This book is also about what to produce, how to produce and for whom to produce. However, the focus here is on the often-overlooked *mental goods* which we recognise to be as important as physical goods. 'Mental goods' are qualities perceived in our minds which are important to our wellbeing, but which do not fill any physical needs. Examples of mental goods are peace of mind, freedom from anxiety, honour, self-esteem, a sense of being accepted by others, sense of success, achieving what we set out to do, self-actualisation and love. Indeed, we know that, across time and space and throughout human existence, people have been killing others and themselves when they feel that they are deprived of an essential mental good. The truly horrific 'honour killing' of tens of thousands of people each year is a case in point. 'Disgrace to the family' is a 'mental bad' – sufficient to cost lives! Even where honour killings are seldom heard of, people may kill or commit suicide when insulted. A wife's extramarital affair may shame the husband so much that he kills the wife or the wife's lover. Suicides due to bullying at school have now acquired the term 'bullycide.'[1] The victims may not be physically bullied at all, but they cannot stand the insults and being ostracised by their peers. Banerjee and Duflo (2012), in a recent highly acclaimed book, documented how the very poor may prefer to suffer hunger and even go into debt in order to pay for an honourable wedding, dowries and funerals.

Thus parents who love their children must not merely procure their physical needs, but also their emotional or mental needs. So mental goods should be produced and procured for those whom we love! But mental goods are quite unlike physical goods, which we can readily buy with money. Mental goods need to be produced by the person who enjoys the mental goods and by those who care for that person – often, but not always, with physical goods acting as a medium. Economics of love is about helping our loved ones acquire the mental goods that they need, and not only procuring the physical goods required for daily maintenance.

An understanding of the importance of mental goods throws light on a number of strange phenomena that are widely considered as irrational (Ariely, 2008). Why are people not happy when they are given a sum of money when they know others get much more than they do? In a 'dictator game', which allows one of the players ('the dictator') to get as big a share as he likes while leaving what is left to the other player, provided that this other player agrees, it is often found that the other player often prefers to reject an unfair division, ending up with nothing for both players. Under the mental goods framework this can be easily explained and is entirely rational. The utility from getting more money is more than offset by the disutility of the mental bad of swallowing an unfair division.

To produce the mental goods that we need, we need to have 'mental capital'. Production of mental goods is not unlike that of physical goods, since both require 'capital' as an input. Formally, capital is a produced means of production. I first introduced the concept of 'mental capital' in my 2001 book *Principles of Public Policy Practice* (Kluwer). Since that time, Rifka Weehuizen has written a doctorate thesis on mental capital in 2008.[2] The UK government, through its Department for Business, Innovation and Skills and Government Office for Science, produced a report on *Mental Capital and Well Being*, later published in a volume edited by Cooper et al. (2009). Cultivating and accumulating mental capital, and clearing away negative mental capital, are two things we need to do ourselves and for our loved ones in order to live a happy, fulfilling life. They are both an act of investment and an act of love.

One interesting and often-overlooked aspect about the differences between mental goods and physical goods is that while the latter is subject to 'the law of diminishing marginal utility' and so 'satiation' is possible the 'law' does not seem to apply to the former. This distinction offers an insight into the paradoxical effect noted by some psychologists, namely that extrinsic rewards sometimes do not work and that they can be counterproductive in motivating people in specific tasks. One classical experiment (Deci, 1975) separated college students into two groups. For one, a monetary reward is paid for solving a puzzle. For the other, no monetary reward is paid, but the students are asked to solve the puzzle in their free time. It turns out that, in repeated experiments, the group that is not paid typically outperforms the group that is paid. They seem to be more interested in the task and to find more satisfaction in solving the puzzle. This result should be seen in the context of the fact that the students taking part in the experiment generally enjoy a degree of relative material abundance. The material reward does not provide that much incentive, and indeed may detract from the mental reward of overcoming the challenge of solving the puzzle.

Imagine that a similar experiment were conducted in another context, this time involving two groups of starving students who live in dire poverty. Because the extrinsic reward becomes much more important, in the sense that marginal utility of the extrinsic reward is in the high rather than the diminished range, we can expect that the group offered the extrinsic reward will work very hard to solve the puzzle. On the other hand, in relatively well-off communities where the monetary reward is no longer as important, the extrinsic reward does not motivate nearly as much, and indeed may signal to players that solving the puzzle is worth no more than the money paid.

Although I seem to have been the first to propose the term mental goods, the concept has been in literature for a long time. Maslow (1954) clearly indicated that there are non-material needs that need to be satisfied. More recently, in the literature on motivation, it has been shown that when an employer demonstrates trust or confidence in an employee, the employee often becomes strongly motivated and will perform better. The knowledge that one is trusted is a mental good that can be quite powerful in motivating people. Thus, quite apart from a pay and benefit package, 'people are motivated by interesting work, challenge, and increasing responsibility—intrinsic factors. People have a deep-seated need for growth and achievement.'[3]

By now there is more and more evidence that happiness is associated with Love, Insight, Fortitude, and Engagement, or LIFE for short – four qualities that reflect the mental capital of a person. Some of this evidence will be reviewed in this book. To be happy, we need to build a capacity to love (Love), a habit of self-reflecting and learning, a realisation that the greatest success in life is making the most out of our own lives, and a sense of proportion (wisdom or Insight), nurturing the strength within ourselves so that we and our loved ones can face adversity without losing heart (Fortitude), and we need to lead an active life with a clear purpose (Engagement). These qualities offer us self-efficacy, optimism, resilience, and hope – the aspects of mental wellbeing that psychologists have come to call 'psychological capital' (Page and Donohue, 2004).

It is sad to see that many within our community need to consume so much of our increasingly scarce resources in order to bolster their wavering and feeble self-esteem and sense of self-dignity. We know that a culture of conspicuous consumption and competition with each other threatens the survival of our own and other species and is really not sustainable. Conspicuous consumption constitutes the single most inefficient (household) production that threatens our very survival, because each time one gains self-dignity by out-consuming others, one's gains are at the same time destroying others' sense of dignity.

Please note that throughout this book I often refer to 'the man' and I use the male pronoun when I mean man or woman. This is entirely for brevity and is not intended for any gender bias.

I hope that this book will contribute a little towards building a happier, more sustainable world.

Lok Sang Ho
Lingnan University
Hong Kong

Notes

1 For statistics, visit: www.bullyingstatistics.org/content/bullying-and-suicide.html.
2 Downloadable from: www.merit.unu.edu/training/theses/Thesis_Weehuizen_final.pdf.
3 See Williams R (2012) Wired for success. How to motivate employees: what managers need to know. *Psychology Today*. Downloadable from: www.psychologytoday.com/blog/wired-success/201210/how-motivate-employees.

Acknowledgements

I thank Dr. Richard Cookerly and Professor Yew-Kwang Ng for writing the forewords, and Andy Chu, who worked as project officer for the Centre for Public Policy Studies from 2012 to 2013, for research assistance. I am also grateful to Centaline Property Agency Ltd., ING Inc., the Early Childhood Development Research Foundation, as well as Lingnan University for funding various studies that provided very important inputs to the current book.

Chapter 1

Introduction to the economics of life

Introduction: economics of life is about making the most out of life

Economics is about making choices amid scarce resources and dilemmas. But life is really the most precious and certainly the scarcest resource for all of us. It is therefore very strange that there is hardly any genuine study of the economics of life in the sense of treating our limited lifespan as a scarce resource and offering a systematic approach to making the most out of our lives.

One reader of an early version of this book objected to this observation, and offered several titles as counterexamples:

- *Freakonomics* and *Superfreakonomics* (Levitt and Dubner, 2005, 2009)
- *The Undercover Economist* (Harford, 2005)/*The Logic of Life* (Harford, 2009)/*The Undercover Economist/Dear Undercover Economist*
- *The Armchair Economist: Economics and Everyday Life* (Landsburg, 2012)
- *The Economic Naturalist: Why Economics Explains Almost Everything* (Frank, 2008)
- Works by Ariely, Cialdini, Thaler and Sunstein.

I had really enjoyed reading *Freakonomics* and had taken delight at reading the Dear Economist column in the *Financial Times* by Tim Harford. However, I see these and most of the others on the list are more in the category of the *economics of everyday life* than in the category of the economics of life. The former tries to explain human behaviour in terms of incentives, and to apply some economic principles to unique situations that we come across in life. The latter, on the other hand, is about viewing life in its entirety as a scarce resource, and confronting human nature as it is, again in its entirety, and finding insight into how we may live a happier, more fulfilling life. Works by Ariely, Cialdini, and Thaler and Sustein are altogether another category. Ariely teaches us about the flaws of human perception; Cialdini tells us how we may be persuaded or motivated; Thaler and Sustein offer advice to policy makers taking human nature as a constraint, trying to justify their brand of 'soft paternalism'. This present volume takes human nature as a constraint and recognises the flaws of human perception, and offers suggestions as to how we can become better masters of ourselves.

A number of articles by Gary Becker had been collected into a book with the title *The Economics of Life: From Baseball to Affirmative Action to Immigration, How Real-World Issues Affect our Everyday Life*, (Becker, 1998) but, again, it is not really about making choices over how we best spend the limited number of years of our lives. To his credit, however, I certainly agree that his theory of allocation of time, published in 1965, is indeed a pioneering study on the economics of life. In that article, he sees various alternative uses of time as competing for the scarce time that individuals have in their command, and trying to optimise given the time constraint.

Typically the life of a person is limited to about 80 years or less. There are centenarians, but there were only around 455,000 centenarians worldwide in 2009, and the global population then was already some 6.8 billion. In the United States male life expectancy at birth is only 76.05 years and that of females is only 81.05 years (2012 estimate). Subtract 12 years from infancy to childhood, and there are only about 68 years of adolescence plus adulthood. Subtract 20 years from infancy to adolescence, and there are only about 60 years of adult life at our disposal. For this short space of 60-plus years, when we can make decisions about our own lives, each day gone is gone forever, and each decision made is *totally irreversible*, in the sense that you can never go back to the time of the decision and make another one. So looking back we may say there is no 'if'. What is done is done. What is done is history, and we have no choice but to take all past decisions as made and given, and to accept whatever consequences came out of those earlier decisions. For good or for ill, we have to live with them.

> Economics is about making the most out of the limited resources that we have – notwithstanding the difficulties that we may face and the misfortunes that could hit us. This book is about making the most of our lives.[1]

Optimising and seeing the big picture

Too many people struggle with making the best decision over something that does not really matter that much in the long run!

Economics is about maximising 'utility', subject to the constraints of limited resources, technology and know-how, law and regulations. 'Making the most' is 'maximising'. Paradoxically, without seeing the big picture and thus without a sense of proportion, trying to 'optimise' could turn out to be counterproductive.

Most people will not lose sleep over which menu they would choose for a dinner, but some will for a banquet for important guests. Many students will have a hard time deciding what programme they will take in university. For the more able ones who face many choices the decision is even harder, as they struggle over whether to study medicine or law or finance (or the like).

These programmes open up different career paths, and they certainly would make a lot of difference on one's life. But unless you go into something that really goes against your personality, so you feel you do not belong there, people can build equally happy, though totally different, careers. It is, of course, natural for people to think about career opportunities and ponder over the possible incomes that these different career paths will bring; however, psychologists and economists now tell us that making more money beyond some threshold does not matter that much to happiness. On the other hand, if you accumulate a good amount of 'mental capital' you may be able to enjoy life regardless of which path you take, and regardless of where you live. Mental capital is an important subject that deserves indepth discussion (see Chapter 4).

Making the most out of our life is a serious matter and has to be taken seriously, but the most important decisions that really determine if our lives will be fulfilling or otherwise pertain to building up life skills. If we have the requisite life skills, many good things follow, because we will then be able to take advantage of opportunities that knock and to weather the storms that may come.

Moreover, being too calculating and overly concerned over marginal comparisons makes us lose sight of *the big picture* (Figure 1.1). Marginal comparisons could bring you up a local hill, but you could be losing big in terms of missing the much higher mountain that yet awaits to be climbed. Even worse, because we do not have perfect information and really do have difficulty meeting the exact optimality conditions, in maximising to the limit we could experience a loss in wellbeing, in terms of the fear of not maximising despite our efforts.

Technically we can say there may be many local maxima, but only one of the maxima is the global maximum. In life especially, there are so many targets that appear appealing at the moment. There is always the temptation to achieve each desirable target as it appears. There are two problems with excessive concern over

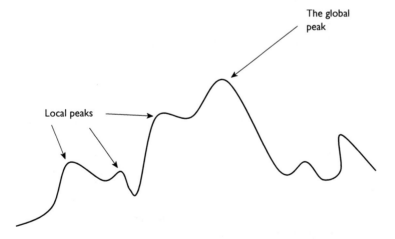

Figure 1.1 Seeing the big picture to truly optimise.

maximising these short-term targets. First is that you could lose sight of an even more attractive target. Second is that if, for some reason, the attempt to achieve it fails, you could be disheartened and lose the spirit to take on other challenges in life. You could dwell upon the failure for too long, and unwittingly give up precious time which is part of your limited life.

In maximising profit, economists advise that, as long as marginal revenue (MR) is larger than marginal cost (MC), i.e., as long as producing an additional unit of a good costs less than the additional revenue it brings in, we should produce more. At profit maximisation, MR would be equal to MC. Similarly, total benefit of a project is maximised by equating the marginal benefit (MB) with the marginal cost (MC) of every quantity that is a decision variable. So one would need to make marginal comparisons in various dimensions in order to maximise. Suppose we run a train service. We have to consider the marginal benefit of extending the hours of service against the marginal cost; the marginal benefit of increasing the frequency of the service at different hours of the day against the marginal cost; and the benefit of extending the distance covered by the train service and that of adding an additional stop. Similarly, there are various decisions in various dimensions that we have to make over different time horizons.

Yet the key to successful living lies in being able to tell what decisions are important and what are not. Most fundamentally, consider life as like a journey. Some people quickly learn to acquire tools and accumulate capital that they could use along the way later. Others take up a lot of junk that would make the journey that much more difficult later on. *The paradoxical truth is that, while they all want to optimise, without knowing it some accumulate positive mental capital, whereas others accumulate negative mental capital.* This leads to totally different qualities of lives.

Cost benefit analysis

There are four principles in the cost benefit analysis that pertains to personal decisions in life. First is the need for discounting future costs and benefits appropriately. Second is that all costs and benefits relevant to decision making need to be forward-looking, i.e. they should be the results of the decisions under consideration. Past benefits and costs do not count. Third is that we have to take account of all the benefits and costs that matter to us, and that includes the benefits and costs that relate to other people whose welfare we care for. Finally we need to recognise that there is always uncertainty in life, so that any cost benefit analysis that we do may be wrong in the end! This however is not a reason for not making an *ex ante* cost benefit comparison in our decisions. Once the decision is made, for good or ill, the decision has been made, and we need to accept the consequences instead of looking back and blaming ourselves for having made a possible error. While learning from past mistakes will make us wiser, excessive regrets may make it difficult to look forward.

There are strong economic reasons behind each of these principles. First, future benefits need to be discounted, not so much because of a pure time preference as such, but because future benefits are subject to uncertainty: we might not even survive, and if we survive, our bodies might not be fit enough to enjoy the contingent benefits. If, say, there is a 5 per cent chance that we might not survive, then the expected benefit should be the possible realisable benefit multiplied by 0.95. Since further into the future, our survival probability declines, benefits further down the road need to be discounted more than benefits that are less far off. But then all discounted future benefits need to be added up into a present value of future contingent benefits.

To be forward-looking in counting the benefits and costs associated with a decision means that we ignore completely the costs or benefits of things that have already happened. We only need to care for the benefits and costs arising from a decision to be made now. Since past benefits and costs are already spent, they cannot be counted as a benefit or cost from a decision or choice at hand.

The third principle says that our decisions could affect others. If we care for or love these other people we should certainly take into consideration the benefits and costs that they derive or incur from our decisions.

The fourth principle says that while we should make the best decision *ex ante*, we can never be certain and should never look back once a decision has been made, except to learn from the experience if there is something to learn or to cherish the memory if there is a memory to cherish. Looking back but not intending to learn from the experience or to cherish the memory is an entire waste of time. If we learn from the experience, we gain mental capital. If we cherish the memory, we enjoy a mental good. If we blame ourselves for having made a wrong decision, we only end up losing more. We would be inflicting a mental bad on ourselves, and losing the chance to build up more mental capital for the future.

When future benefits and costs are 'discounted' to obtain a 'present value' that is comparable to today's benefits and costs, the choice of the discount rate would make a huge difference and would affect the ranking of different options open to us. Those whose discount rate is very high would tend to ignore investing for future benefits, since future benefits do not count as much as present benefits. They are more likely to smoke, for example, even though they know that smoking may lead to poor health in the future. In general, in countries where life expectancy is low, such as countries where there is much violence or a civil war, the chances of surviving into old age are low, and future benefits will be discounted heavily. But the implied behaviour when one adopts a high discount rate would actually lead to a lower life expectancy. Although their lifestyle such as smoking and unsafe sex may not have any obvious immediate effect on 'functional health' – their ability to carry out day-to-day functions is not impaired – it may hurt the 'health stock' and reduce their life expectancy (Ho, 2012). Thus life expectancy is 'endogenously determined' rather than given exogenously. In general, people who treasure their lives and look forward to living a long life will adopt a low discount rate for future benefits, and they would actively pursue a lifestyle that will help bring about a long life.

Household production, physical goods and mental goods

Economists generally assume that consumers maximise utility. Over the last half-century, the term household is increasingly used in place of the word consumer, and the concept of household production is fast replacing the concept of consumption, at least in microeconomic theory. Gary Becker's truly seminal paper, 'A theory of allocation of time' (1965), can be said to be the first and one of very few papers on the economics of life. He argues that utility, instead of being directly dependent on goods and services purchased in the market place, depends on 'basic commodities' (his terminology) or 'end goods' that must be produced by the household, often with various market goods or services as some of the inputs, in combination with time inputs through various household activities (Figure 1.2). Moreover, households are seen to supply labour, and they can potentially work more to increase their income. For those who can work more to earn more, then, income is not given. There is thus no 'fixed budget' constraint as such. On the other hand, time is a real constraint. The more one works, the less time one will have after work. Under the time constraint, the more one works, the more income one enjoys, but the time worked translates into less time available for household activities. Becker highlighted the trade-off between work and leisure, as people give up earnings in favour of more leisure or free time, which they need in order to procure the 'end goods' that they need to enjoy life. This pertains to the important subject of work–life balance, now a hot subject in psychology.

While using Becker's concept of household production, this book stresses that *end goods* that affect people's wellbeing comprise *mental goods* as well as *physical (end) goods*. Mental goods include a long list of things that we value, including a sense of autonomy, freedom from anxiety, being respected and

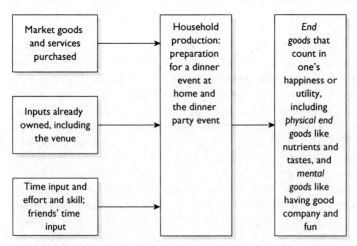

Figure 1.2 Household production.

being accepted by others, a sense of security, self-esteem, sense of accomplishment, and self-actualisation. Much of this was discussed by Abraham Maslow (1954) in the context of human hierarchy of wants. Maslow proposed that physical needs are more basic, which seems obvious as people will die of starvation but do not die because of a lack of self-esteem. But we also know that people could kill themselves or others if they are shamed. We know that in some countries and among some people the horrific practice of 'honour killing' is considered legitimate. In the United States we heard of a very sad story of a student at Rutgers University killing himself in 2010 when his sexual activity in the dorm was secretly video-recorded by his roommate and broadcast on the internet. Which are more basic, physical or mental needs, is thus really not as obvious as may be thought. Just as a failure to procure a minimum of physical goods kills, so does a failure to procure a minimum of mental goods. Mental goods are just as important as physical goods to human existence.[2]

Among the mental goods, loving and being loved are two of the most important that enrich people's lives significantly and make them meaningful.[3] Although a lack of financial resources may lead to many 'mental bads' like anxiety and insecurity, some of the mental goods cannot be acquired simply by expending more, and loving and being loved are two of the things that money cannot buy. This explains why some rich people who can get all the physical goods and services that they want – including caring services – are still unhappy. A nurse hired to care for you, even when the care is meticulous and well executed, is no substitute for loving care from one's family.

Mental goods are also related to 'prospective happiness' and 'retrospective happiness'. When someone is very much looking forward to something that is expected to happen, one may be full of energy and anticipation. The anticipated event has not yet happened, but it is sufficient to make one very happy now. Similarly, when someone looks back and cherishes fond memories of things that happened in the past, one may also feel sweetness and contented. Just as a future happy event can make one happy, so a future unhappy event can engender fear and anxiety. Just as a past happy event can make one happy now, so a past unhappy event can make one depressed, regretful or traumatised.

Mental goods and motivation

The fact that human beings value mental goods a lot is well recognised in everyday life, although economists tend to ignore them in their formal analysis, which is a pity. Failing to recognise the importance of mental goods, economists tend to place an excessive emphasis on material incentives. Singapore pays its senior civil servants and ministers the world's highest salaries, because it is believed that money will attract the best people to serve the country. If the CEOs of top corporations are paid around $x, to be commensurate with the private sector and if the country's prime minister is considered the CEO for the country, then certainly the pay has to be commensurate with private-sector pay in order to be competitive, so goes the logic. However, many outstanding people are willing and happy to render their services and even make huge sacrifices without demanding a huge pay package. This is because they can achieve the mental good of knowing that they are serving the country.

Mental goods then have much to do with 'intrinsic motivation'. While a good pay package is usually considered to provide an extrinsic motivation, a decent pay package also offers a mental good in the form of knowing that one is well treated and that one's contribution is well recognised. People may accept a small pay package working for someone who they know cannot afford to pay more if they can get job satisfaction, but are unlikely to accept an unfairly small pay package working for someone who can well afford to pay at the market rate.

Mental goods therefore are not completely divorced from material goods or money, which represents command over material goods. Material goods or money often provide a medium to create or destroy mental goods. Excessively low pay may signal to employees that they are not well appreciated by the employer, which is a mental bad. On the other hand, mental goods sometimes need not require a material good or money as a medium. The trust that an employer expresses to employees may be sufficient to motivate them to perform better. On the other hand, distrust could ruin their motivation and undermine their performance.

While intrinsic motivations often are even more effective than extrinsic motivations, much depends on the circumstances of the worker. For someone who desperately needs money, extrinsic motivation may be quite effective. But for those who do not really need the money so badly, paying money to get things done could be counterproductive, because this could signal that the worker was just working for the money. Benabou and Tirole (2003) cited the experiment of Deci (1975) that showed that college students paid to do a puzzle were less motivated and less engaged than those who are not paid, suggesting that the pay could 'debase' the value of an activity.

Ageing and the economics of life

One of the key aspects of the economics of life is that decisions are made at some points in one's life, and that once made they are completely irreversible. Life is fleeting, and with each day gone we inevitably grow older, and we can never go back to the time of the initial decision. In the event that we regret our earlier decision, we still have to take that as already done. We can at most try to figure out what is the best thing to do given the foregone decision. With ageing, our physique changes and our health conditions change. Second, our values and our perspective on life change. Third, we have become 'experienced' in many things. Fourth, our brains have been programmed in such a way that we have acquired certain patterns of thinking and behaviour from which it is difficult to deviate. What and how we have learnt would even make it more difficult for us to learn new things. As a result of all of these things, our *household production functions* change. It will be useful for us to be aware of these laws of ageing early in life, so that we can achieve what gerontologists call 'successful ageing'.

Successful ageing consists of several elements: maintaining our physical and mental health in top form as far as possible by reducing the rate of depreciation of the health stock (Ho, 2012). This requires adopting a healthy, active and purposive lifestyle *early in life* physically, mentally and socially. Interestingly, the brain does not depreciate but rather improves with use.[4] Prevention would be too late if it is begun late! Regret is of no use and is even counterproductive. Adopting the right lifestyle and attitude early in life is probably the most important message from the economics of life.

Conclusions

We are distinct individuals in that our personality and traits are quite different. Our genes are different and we come from different backgrounds. Yet we share many things in common. Despite the differences, we have very similar needs and similar emotions, to the extent that translation from any language to any other is possible. It is often pointed out that needs are different from wants. Wants are supposed to be things that we can do without, but actually many of the things that 'we can do without' fill a real 'mental good' need.

Most people who opt for plastic surgery do not 'need' the plastic surgery physically. But they spend huge amounts and often go through much trouble and even physical pain to receive the plastic surgery. We certainly have no physical need for jewellery, but attending some occasions without any jewellery could make some women feel very bad, and it could be like men attending functions without a tie and a suit when all the other men are wearing them. All these cases may comprise mental goods involving a perception of 'acceptance by others' and that of 'self-acceptance'. Perhaps it is more accurate to say that there are many different ways of filling similar needs. Some ways are far more costly than others. But for some people their mentality is such that they can only get their mental good needs fulfilled in specific ways that may prove very costly. We will explore what determines this mentality in the next two chapters.

Another similarity that we all share is the laws of nature that govern us. We all grow old, and we share very similar emotions, to the extent that the vocabularies of totally different languages are strikingly similar. In every language and culture that we know there is a word for anger, for jealousy, for love, for sorrow and for pain. As we look back into history, events that are long gone stir similar emotions even today, and all the literature that depicts different aspects of humanity continues to find resonance today.

Recognising our common constraints, the laws that govern our physical and emotional lives and trying to make the most out of our limited lives given those constraints is thus the most rational thing to do. It appears self-evident that the economics of life is an economics for everybody.

Notes

1 A recent French movie, *Declaration of War*, told the story of a couple taking the hard reality of their newborn baby afflicted by brain cancer cheerfully and making the most out of their lives through love and wisdom.
2 For this reason putting some limits to freedom of speech appears to be well justified – speech that sets out to hurt other people's feelings causes the victims to suffer a loss in mental goods. A potentially dangerous situation could arise when such loss is big enough. Some fatal campus shootings in the United States have been attributed to unfair treatment or mockery by others.
3 Love here is defined as a yearning and caring from the heart for the wellbeing of the one who is loved. It is distinguished from 'romantic love'. A discussion about this distinction will be given in the next chapter.
4 Dana Alliance for Brain Initiatives and the NRTA (2009) offer an introduction to neuroscience and some very good tips for successful ageing.

Chapter 2

Love and the economics of love

Introduction

Gary Becker (1965) pointed out that 'utility' does not come about simply by purchasing market goods and services. Similarly, Kelvin Lancaster (1966) suggested that consumers are not really interested in the goods bought in the market *per se* but are looking for certain 'characteristics' offered by the goods. What Becker called 'basic commodities', Lancaster called 'characteristics'. Both Becker and Lancaster attempt to go behind the market goods to discover what really matters to utility. It was Becker, however, who pioneered the concept of *household production*. In contrast, Lancaster thought the 'characteristics' of goods were inherent in the goods purchased.

Unfortunately, both Becker and Lancaster missed one really important point – that 'utility' is not derived from 'physical attributes' or 'physical characteristics' alone. Life would be too dreary if 'value' were derived only by people acting like consumption machines that gobble up goods and services in the market place. Unfortunately, this has been the mainstream economics doctrine. Nobel Laureate J.R. Hicks (1939) titled his highly acclaimed book *Value and Capital: An Inquiry into some Fundamental Principles of Economic Theory*, and the focus of his analysis was the consumption of goods purchased in the market place. Hicks laid much of the foundations of microeconomics as it is known today, by clarifying the distinction between the 'income effect' and the 'substitution effect' of a price change. If the price of a good falls, it saves the consumer money, which then acts like an increase in income, which tends to boost the consumption of all goods. This is the *income effect*. At the same time, because the price has fallen, it has become more attractive to buy this good rather than another good. This is the *substitution effect*. But value certainly goes beyond the goods and services that money can buy; and the value of the goods and services that money can buy is not derived just from the physical attributes associated with those goods. Those who are familiar with marketing know very well that consumers are in pursuit of *mental goods* as well. For example, marketing professionals try very hard to have potential consumers associate certain products with a glamorous lifestyle, self-confidence and success. Most advertising does very little in conveying to consumers the physical qualities of the products. Instead it usually focuses on glamour, confidence, style, recognition, caring, love – all of which are mental goods.

An important observation about mental goods is that, although physical goods sometimes serve as inputs in producing the mental goods, physical goods cannot really substitute for mental goods. For example, a life full of love is a fulfilling one. So love is clearly a mental good. But even though money can buy care in the market place, it cannot buy love from those for whom one cares, such as one's children or spouse; nor does money buy a loving heart. Some people are incapable of loving and may have seldom experienced love. They can be quite rich and yet unhappy, because all the physical goods that money can buy may not bring them love. While some mental goods are easier to obtain – for example, through the purchase of an insurance policy one can enjoy greater peace of mind being protected against some feared scenarios – the capacity to love has to be nurtured and cultivated over a long period of time, and can only come naturally in an environment that is favourable to its natural development.

Mental goods as outputs of household production

Why do people pay hundreds of times more on one watch rather than another one, when the other one can tell time just as well and may even have many more functions? One might say it is more beautiful. But is it really the more beautiful design that makes it command that much higher a price? If the answer is yes, how can we explain the huge effort made on designing an advertisement to promote it? Why is 'brand building' so vital in marketing?

In an affluent society people are particularly used to using commercial goods as a means to acquire mental goods and to deliver mental goods to others. A bundle of flowers on Valentine's day may convey one's care and love for one's lover. On Mother's day and Father's day, and on someone's graduation, as well as many other occasions, an appropriately designed card with nice words carries a message of love, celebration or congratulation. The cards that people receive are of absolutely no use, and certainly do not fill any of their physical needs, but they deliver mental goods, which make the physical objects (a card or a gift) very much treasured. When a couple in love go to a movie or a concert together, the movie or the concert could be secondary. The mental good derived from spending an evening together may be far more important.

But mental goods do not always have to cost anything. A letter may not cost anything in money terms, but the mental good delivered to the recipient may be far greater than that delivered by a card that costs quite a few dollars, though it takes time to write and the person may not even write very well. Kind words and encouragement also do not cost anything, but they may be deeply appreciated and may even change a person's life. Being together with someone we love and walking casually and relaxing in the park or along the lakeshore could be very nice, and it need not cost anything. But over the ages there have been many sceptics about love without lavish spending. To wit:

> Daisy, Daisy, give me your answer true!
> I'm half crazy, all for the love of you;
> It won't be a stylish marriage.
> I can't afford a carriage.
> But you'll look sweet upon the seat of
> a bicycle made for two.

> Michael, Michael, this is my answer true:
> I can't cycle half as well as you;
> If you can't afford a carriage,
> there'll be no bloomin' marriage,
> For I'll be blowed if I'll be towed
> On a bicycle made for two.

The fact remains, however, that there are costly and not so costly ways of procuring mental goods. There are limits to how much or how many physical needs people have to fill, but there is virtually no limit as to how much one can spend to procure the mental goods that we need. The efficiency of the household production function varies greatly from person to person. By efficiency is meant the output-to-input ratio. Spending a lot but getting little out of the spending is inefficient. As we will see in the next chapter, the efficiency of household production in generating mental goods has much to do with culture. *Culture plays a key role in the economics of life*.[1]

Mahatma Gandhi has been quoted as having said: 'There's enough for everybody's need and not for anybody's greed.' But we do not have to be moralistic in interpreting people's 'greedy' behaviour. In a sense we are all the same, in that we all have similar mental good needs, even though we are vastly different in our efficiency of procuring them. We all want to be respected and accepted by those we associate with. We all want peace of mind and freedom from anxiety. We all want a sense of freedom and autonomy, and do not like being told what to do and what not to do. We all want to feel strong and dignified. We all want love and 'self-actualisation': discovering and realising the potential that lies within in our different ways. The challenge is how we can procure all of this, without leaving too much ecological footprint, so that our needs can all be fulfilled and that the fulfilment of these needs today will not undermine the fulfilment of the same needs for our progeny.

Nature of love

This brings us back to the subject of love. In this book love strictly refers to *a yearning from inside to realise the best that life can offer for those for whom we care*, including ourselves. I would not distinguish the love between a couple 'in love' from the love between parents and children. I would regard the romantic passion between a couple 'in love' as distinct from the love between them. John who loves Mary from his heart expresses that love through a genuine concern for the wellbeing of Mary and a readiness to offer *emotional support* whenever needed. Rick who 'loves' Mary passionately just wants her to be at his side and treats her like something that he possesses. John could sacrifice his life for Mary if this sacrifice would somehow help Mary go through difficult times. Rick could kill himself if Mary rejects him. I would define the former as love and call the latter simply an *obsessive possessiveness*.

Love: a blessing from the heart

Have a Reverence for Life, loving yourself as much as you would love others.
Love starts with loving yourself . . . your life . . .
Then extending to your immediate family . . .
Then extending to all forms of life.

Love is an aspiration from deep inside:
An aspiration that the loved one will live a life free from worry;
A wish that the loved one will realize one's full potential and will enjoy a rich life:
Away from danger and ever joyful.

A pure love is free from self-interest considerations;
A broad-minded love benefits all;
An enduring love is ever so new;
A selfless love knows no sacrifice too big.
Love always stems from identifying with Life.
    There are no other kinds of Love.

Love is unconditional and certainly not an exchange.
Love requires nothing in return.
Love is the strongest motive.
Love often begins with a relationship.
Yet it must transcend that relationship.
    Love is a Blessing from the Heart.

(Ho, 2012)

Box 2.1 Major elements of love

High valuing – hold in high esteem, see as of much merit, prize, treasure, cherish, respect, appreciate, affirm the worth of, admire, assess as important, hold precious, see as fine, excellent, matchless, superior, uniquely fitting, incomparable, special. Healthy real love consistently highly values the loved.

Powerful – strong, vigorous, mighty, indomitable, potent, forceful, influential, effectual, energy-filled, dynamic, ascendant, prevailing. Healthy real love is amazingly powerful.

Vital – important to life, necessary to life process and function, alive, viable, of paramount importance to continued existence, thriving, having to do with the life force and its cardinal process, a biological, neuro-chemical, psycho-neuro-physiological phenomenon. Healthy real love is a great, vital force for healthy life.

Natural – of nature, part of essential existence, inherently of fundamental reality, intrinsically part of the cosmos, especially essential to the processes of nature and natural existence, in life a biological, neuro-chemical, psycho-socio-neuro-physiological phenomenon.

We are naturally constructed to thrive via love.

Process – an active succession of systematic, changing operations with a developing progressive, onward organized flow. Healthy real love is a growth process.

Desiring for the well-being of the loved – wishing and wanting for the loved to live well, be well, do well, be happy and thrive; and when not so doing wanting the loved to return to well-being.

Acting for the well-being of the loved – behaving often or when possible to nurture, protect, assist, support, affirm, heal, cause improvement and otherwise promote the well-being of the loved.

Taking pleasure in the well-being of the loved – experiencing joy, happiness and many other positive emotions when the loved is perceived as doing well, thriving, succeeding, growing, healthfully happy and ascendant; this often involves pleasure sharing with the loved.

Well-being – a state of thriving, championed by those who love healthfully; the absence of a loved one's well-being is threatening to those who love and the absence is a consistent motivation to assist, when needed or useful, the continuance of well-being.

(source: whatislovedrcookerly.com/
97/the-definition-of-love/, courtesy of Richard Cookerly)

Relational psychotherapist J. Richard Cookerly defined love thus[2]: 'Healthy real love is a powerful, vital, natural process of highly valuing, desiring for, often acting for, and taking pleasure in the well-being of the loved.'

This definition corresponds to mine. It is nice to see that a relational psychotherapist sees love along the same lines as I do. He points out that true love involves a respect for life and is a truly potent force, and that true love is spontaneous and natural. Box 2.1 shows an excerpt from his website. Although love is natural and spontaneous, it can be overpowered by other equally potent forces, in particular *egocentrism* and *possessiveness*. But even the most egocentric and possessive person needs to be loved. This is why some very rich people are unhappy notwithstanding their huge wealth. Without love one may feel lonely, betrayed, insecure and angry, and lacking in self-esteem, and by definition money cannot buy love. Money certainly can buy care from a commercial caregiver, but if the care is purchased you know deep in your heart this is not love. Rich people can get all the care they need by paying for it, but they will still be yearning for that someone who cares for them from the heart.

Thus love is one of the very crucial 'mental goods' that enrich one's life and make life meaningful and thus worth living. Indeed love is a very strong driving force, not only for individuals in pursuit of their dreams, but also for the transformation of society and in particular the economy (Richard and Rudnyckyj, 2009).

Love without excessive attachment

Love as discussed here is to be distinguished from 'romantic love', which social psychologist Zick Rubin (1970) says is characterised by:

1 Attachment: The need to be cared for and be with the other person. This encompasses a desire for physical contact and approval by this other person.
2 Caring: Valuing the other person's happiness and needs as much as one's own.
3 Intimacy: Sharing private thoughts, feelings and desires with the other person.

Rubin developed a Romantic Love Scale based on responses to 13 questions, which fall under the above three categories. As readers can see, 'caring' in the sense of *caring from the heart*[3] is one of the three hallmarks of romantic love according to Rubin, and this is no different from true love under our earlier definition. But Rubin additionally requires *attachment* and *intimacy* as telling signs of romantic love. Consider his questionnaire, from which the love scale is to be derived. Respondents are asked to answer to what degree they agree to the following statements:

- I find it easy to ignore his (her) faults.
- I feel very possessive toward him (her).

- If I could never be with him (her), I would feel miserable.
- It would be hard for me to get along without him (her).
- When I am with him (her), I spend a good deal of time just looking at him (her).
- I would do almost anything for him (her).

Being attached to and feeling possessive about a person who has attracted one's romantic love is quite natural. A degree of attachment is not only natural, but may be very healthy for developing healthy interpersonal relations. In particular, physical contact and intimacy are very effective in communicating love and support. This is as true for parental love as for the love between two spouses. But *excessive* attachment goes counter to the purpose of true love: you would not want the one whom you truly love to be too attached to you, since excessive attachment diminishes the possibilities that one can make out of one's life. You would also like your beloved one to have the courage and the ability to live and thrive even without you. Excessive attachment is unfortunately often highlighted in romantic dramas, and *Romeo and Juliet* is an example of a Shakespearean tragedy founded on excessive attachment. We really should break the often taken-for-granted but totally misguided notion that greater is the love when the attachment is greater.

Loving economically

Economists talk of the diminishing utility of a good. Within a time period, the more a good is consumed, the smaller becomes the marginal utility – the utility derived from an additional unit of consumption. As far as physical goods are concerned, this is clearly true. There is only so much food that can be eaten; only so much clothing that can be worn; only so much accommodation that one can call a home. Our lives are finite, so the claim for 'insatiable wants' would not make much sense if only physical goods matter. Some may counterargue that there is no limit to the quality of the physical goods that can be coveted. But in truth, such clamour for *ever higher* quality is often more in the nature of a clamour for a mental good, such as an assertion that one is satisfied with only having the best products.[4] Knowing and letting others know that they are getting the best that is available makes them feel good.

Many of us have heard of the Taj Mahal story. The Taj Mahal was built in the seventeenth century by the fifth Mughal emperor and grandson of Akbar the Great, Shah Jahan, in memory of his beloved wife Mumtaz Mahal, who died giving birth to their 14th child. The construction was said to have taken 22,000 workers, toiling 22 years. The Taj Mahal did not fill a physical need of the loved person nor that of the lover, but rather a mental need. The emperor wanted to tell the world how much he loved Mahal, or, more romantically, he wanted to tell the dead Mahal how much he loved her. His mind would not be at peace until the most beautiful monument in the world was built in her memory.

The Taj Mahal story may suggest that the love between a couple is not the same as the love between, say, a mother and a child, or that between two siblings, or that between two friends. Surely the way love is expressed may vary from one relationship to another, but this does not really detract from the universal nature of true love, regardless of the relationship, which is the desire for the loved one to live a good life, to live in peace, to die in peace, and to enjoy eternal bliss, if that is possible.

I have observed that 'Love often begins with a relationship. Yet it must transcend that relationship.' When true love is lighted up between a couple 'in love', the partner who is loved becomes a person to the true lover and is recognised as a person, just as the child who is truly loved by his/her parent (biological or adopted) is recognised as a person. The true lover, regardless of the relationship, will be prepared to make sacrifices for the loved person for his/her benefit. When the love is sufficiently strong the true lover may even lay down his/her life for the loved one.

It is indeed rare that a father would build a Taj Mahal for his daughter, but building a Taj Mahal for one's deceased wife is also quite rare. And there are fathers (or mothers) who buy a car or a house for their daughter just as there are husbands (or wives) who buy a car or a house for their wife (or husband).

But you would agree with me that building a Taj Mahal or buying a car or a house is really not a requirement in love. Indeed, excessively pampering the loved person is often not the best way to love the person. The economics of love tells us that we need to love effectively and efficiently. We would be loving effectively if the acts of love produce the intended effect of enhancing the wellbeing of the beloved. We would be loving efficiently if we can make the most out of what we have to enhance the wellbeing of the beloved. Excessively pampering the loved person is neither an effective nor an efficient way of loving that person. You can spoil a spouse just as you can spoil a child.

In contrast to spending big, taking delight in simple things can often bring huge rewards. There are many things that people do: taking a walk in the park, watching birds, star gazing, listening to music, singing, calligraphy, writing a poem, writing a diary, making bread, taking pictures, playing chess, playing table tennis, swimming, flower arrangement, learning to play a musical instrument. Some of this list could be expensive too, but most need not be that expensive. Many of these things we can do with our beloved ones; others we can do alone. But all the same, they add colour to our lives, and often food for conversation, and fun. The interesting thing is that most people do not realise that they have certain talents which they are not aware of. Being involved and getting active allow us to rediscover ourselves.

Although the title for this section is 'Loving economically', when the time comes for spending big, such as when big spending really can improve the quality of life, saving money would be the last thing in the mind of the true lover, since compared to life money will always be secondary. 'Loving economically' means maximising the welfare of the beloved given whatever resources available. Since money is only a means to an ends, money is never to be saved at the expense of the welfare of the beloved.

Interspousal spillovers and division of labour

But 'the beloved' should include both the lover and the loved. A lover can love others only if he loves himself. If he does not know how to love himself, and if he does not love himself, it is not possible for him to love others effectively, i.e. bring happiness to the loved ones.

So, in the case of a couple who truly loves each other, whether they are husband and wife or a common-law couple, economically loving would require maximising the welfare of the couple with the resources available. This generally would require a division of labour between the couple to enhance the welfare of both. As is often pointed out, this would require specialisation according to comparative advantage. Comparative advantage does not mean that whoever can do a job better than the other will take up that job. Suppose the husband is actually a better cook than the wife. It does not follow that he should take charge of the cooking. The key question is if the husband has limited time to spend, which is the better way to spend the time: cooking or mending the roof? Suppose the wife cannot mend the roof; naturally she should cook and the husband should mend the roof. Suppose the husband can cook or make money. The wife can also do both jobs, but can cook relatively better than making money; then following the principle of comparative advantage she should cook, and the husband should make money.

Now suppose it is cooking time and the husband prefers making music to cooking, and making music means a lot to the husband. What should the wife do? If she really loves him, she should still do the cooking, since the wife cannot do anything else to make her husband nearly as happy as when he makes music. Conversely, the husband may take up certain jobs in the house to let his wife do something that she really enjoys.

Apart from division of labour, emotional support and sharing of learning are also important in a love relationship. In Chapter 4 we will discuss at length the concept of mental capital. At this point it is sufficient to point out that each person owns some 'mental capital' that could be a true asset but could also be a liability, depending on whether that mental capital is positive or negative. In general, someone with strong positive mental capital is better able to offer emotional support, advice and other forms of help to his spouse. For that reason, being married to someone with a lot of mental capital is a real blessing, because the person will enjoy the positive spillover from the marriage partner. Being married to one who has much less mental capital or even a lot of negative mental capital could be a pain. But the challenge then is to turn him or her around, and to nurture whatever positive mental capital there is while helping him or her overcome the negative mental capital.

Attracting love and 'tough love'

If love is intended to improve the quality of life of the beloved, it is important to nurture love in the beloved, since the evidence shows that someone who does not know love is unlikely to live a fulfilling life. In order to nurture love, not only is it necessary to offer the person whom you love things that offer utility, such as good food, but also what may appear to offer disutility, such as hard work. Asking children to share some of the household work is an example, and this should be done at an early age, before they have learned to refuse. Young children will not be able to do things that require strength and skill, and may not do well what they are asked to do, but that is not important. What is important is for them to learn that sharing the housework is the natural thing to do. It is important not to reprimand them for doing a bad job. Quite the contrary, even if they do not do as well we should give them encouragement and should recognise their effort. Such words of encouragement and recognition provide a mental reward. By seeing how difficult it is to do a good job, they will learn to appreciate what other people do for them. This is the idea of 'tough love'.

Asking children to share the housework sometimes becomes a problem, since they may complain about 'uneven sharing of the workload'. This is potentially a problem with siblings who could be overly concerned about 'fairness'. Remembering that a sense of unfairness is a mental bad, reprimanding them for this is not very effective. Instead, countering with teaching by example – showing one's readiness to help without worrying if one has done more than one's fair share, and offering a mental good in the form of encouragement or appreciation for an uncalculating attitude – will work, especially when the children are still young.

Some parents pay children to do housework. This has both advantages and disadvantages. Working for pay is the way of the market, and children will have to learn the ways of the market sooner or later. However, within a family where love is treasured, the way of the market is not really the most appropriate.

Children need to learn to take work as driven by a desire to do good, and particularly by love. A loving person attracts love when he goes about his day-to-day activities thinking about doing good to others and to himself. As Erich Fromm (1956) explains in *The Art of Loving*, self-love is really synonymous with loving one's own life and this is a precondition for loving others. Parents who know self-love will inspire self-love in the children. The corollary, obviously, is that parents who do not love themselves will *never* inspire self-love in their children. Loving parents will *always* inspire love in their children, even though patience will be needed. A seed, provided it is alive, will *always* germinate under the necessary conditions, but there has to be sufficient time for the germination to take place. Similarly, a loving husband/wife will inspire love from his/her spouse. Human emotions are such that they tend to attract and draw out the same kind. In psychology there is already a huge literature on *emotional contagion*. So hate does beget hate, and love begets love.[5] This is a constraint that rational decision makers have to accept as a fact of life.

Doing something side by side (such as working on the house or working on a fun project), enjoying something side by side (e.g. singing, cooking, hiking), learning something side by side (learning a musical instrument, for example) is an aspect of sharing. All of this sharing – sharing working together and sharing the fun together – can be looked upon as an investment in mental capital. From time to time parents may share their insights with children, and marriage partners can share their insights with each other on life and on other things. In this way they are companions in their life journeys.

It is common for parents to save the best foods and best everything for their children. But we need to resist this, and instead insist that sharing is natural and good.

Self-love

Learning to love oneself is the best way to learn how to love others effectively. This is an example of *learning by doing*. To the extent that human beings are tied by a common bond and share broadly similar characteristics, if we know how to love and take care of ourselves we also know how to love and take care of others. This is why both western and eastern cultures teach, 'Don't do unto others what you don't want others to do unto you.'

In this connection consider the case of addiction. Consumption of addictive goods like tobacco, alcohol and drugs is very common, and some behaviours like gambling and computer games are also found to be addictive. Becker and Murphy (1988) came up with the idea of 'rational addiction', and stipulate that the goods are addictive because consumption of these goods leads to the accumulation of 'addictive capital' or 'addictive stock'. This 'addictive capital' is obviously a 'negative capital', as it undermines the addict's long-term welfare. The central tenet of their paper is that, while the addictive stock momentarily increases utility rises from the consumption, it has a negative impact on utility over the longer run. The 'rational addict' has to find an optimal trade-off between the benefit from the short-term gain and the cost from the longer-term loss. The reduction in marginal utility over the longer run is due to increasing tolerance – a kind of 'adaptation' or getting used to the excitement so that what excites becomes less exciting. However, Becker and Murphy ignored or forgot the sense of loss of autonomy that afflicts the addict. This sense of loss of autonomy is a truly serious 'mental bad'. Addicts discover that they are 'hooked', and that when the time comes for another thrill there is little they can do but surrender to the biological clock that tells them this is the time for another intake of the substance. Typically, we find addicts frustrated with their loss of autonomy and therefore unhappy. Self-love would require steering oneself away from addictive substances.

Consider the related case of adopting a healthy lifestyle. This is important to ward off or postpone the onset of diseases that can debilitate or kill us. A healthy lifestyle is actually most effective when adopted at a young age. When our health stock has already been more or less depleted, prevention would be too late. But young people may not be aware of the adverse consequences of an unhealthy lifestyle, because they do not notice any immediate effect on their health.

Thus self-love requires a forward-looking perspective. When we can take good care of ourselves, we help our beloved ones to do the same by example.

Conclusions

The economics of love is about how to love effectively and efficiently, and a starting point of this is to understand that human beings do not live on bread alone, and to realise that our lives and those of our dear ones are the most valuable things in the world. We need to know that there are mental good needs as well as physical good needs. Both needs have to be fulfilled for one to live a happy, fulfilled life. If you love someone – whether that someone is your lover, your spouse, your child or your friend – you care for his/her mental good needs as much as his/her physical needs, and you would like to love most efficiently and effectively given the limited span of your and his/her lives and the resources available. The resources include not only financial resources, but also the capability that one has accumulated over the years in the form of skills, wisdom and temperament, and the time invested in cultivating and nurturing this capability.

Notes

1 Room *et al.* (2001) suggest that mental bads such as stigmatisation related to disability may also vary with, and be conditioned by, culture.
2 See Cookerly (2001) for further elaboration.
3 There certainly are non-loving caregivers who 'care' for the cared as part of their jobs or routines.
4 Yew-Kwang Ng coined the term 'diamond good' to describe goods that are treasured because they are considered high-quality and precious. Paying a premium price on diamond goods makes the consumer feel good because the high price creates a perception of higher quality. For a discussion, see Deng and Ng (2004).
5 It is interesting to observe that psychologists Hatfield *et al.* cited Adam Smith in their 1993 article.

Chapter 3

The role of culture in household production

Introduction: nature of culture

It is a pity that modern economics takes culture and values as given. As a result, each individual is considered as a 'utility-maximising' decision maker given his values and culture. This approach is fine if we want to explain how people behave, but counterproductive if we want to make the most of our lives.

Actually, the most important choices in life relate to choices about culture and value. The economics of life distinguishes from the economics of everyday life in that it confronts cultural choices explicitly.

We have learnt that there is no right and wrong about culture and values. We agree that there is nothing inherently good or bad about culture and values. But to the extent that different norms and values lead to different wellbeing outcomes, and that we care about wellbeing outcomes, we need to be choosy about culture and values. Most cultural practices and norms that are associated with ethnicity do not matter much with regard to such outcomes and do deserve our respect, but cultural influences such as excessive materialism and competition will undermine the quality of our lives.

Culture consists of all the implicit norms and values and ways in which people conduct their lives. Take what we eat, for example. Pork is eaten by many people but not by Muslims or Jews. Jews only eat kosher foods which excludes many foodstuffs, some of which must be prepared in specific ways in order to be kosher, as instructed in the book of Leviticus. In some communities, spiders, scorpions and worms are delicacies, which would be unthinkable in other communities. Take how we clothe ourselves, as another example. Certain kinds of attire would be perfectly acceptable in some societies but utterly unacceptable in others. Despite all the differences, however, all human beings have to eat and they need essentially the same nutrients in order to stay healthy; and all human beings need to be dressed in such a way as to be acceptable in their respective communities, and to be clothed to protect against cold and heat.

People of different cultural and ethnic backgrounds may eat differently, dress differently, worship differently, communicate with one another in different languages and they may live in different kinds of housing. But despite all the differences, they are all human beings and are subject to the same physical and psychological laws that govern their lives as humans. We procure our different needs in different ways, but we share similar needs, emotions and aspirations. Although there are shades of meanings that are different, all languages surprisingly have similar words that convey very similar meanings, so that translations of novels, poems and speeches are possible and meaningful. Moreover, apart from the new words that have appeared in recent years on account of the technological revolution, most of the vocabulary that we have today has existed for a long time, even though the words might be in a different form.

Human nature is by and large universal, the diversity of cultures and ethnicities notwithstanding.

It is important to note that culture crucially affects how we procure our needs, both mental and physical. Using the terminology of Becker, we buy various goods and services in the market place, and through 'household production' turns them into various 'basic commodities'(my preferred terminology is 'end goods') that enhance our wellbeing. My extension of Becker's hypothesis is that these 'end goods' include both mental and physical goods, and that the technology of our household production or *household production functions* is conditioned by our cultural backgrounds and our past activities. More about the contribution of activities to household production function will be discussed in the next chapter. The effect of culture on household production can be seen readily by looking at the way people of different cultural backgrounds prepare and cook their food. Indeed, what are foods to non-Jewish people may not even be considered to be foods by Jews. More importantly, however, is how different people procure the mental goods that they need. This is because the resource implications of the different ways people procure their physical needs are not nearly as huge as those of the different ways people procure their mental needs.

The culture of the *nouveau riche*

In this context culture does not just refer to ethnoculture, but also the culture of groups of people living and interacting with one another closely. China is now known to be a rapidly emerging luxury good market, and many Chinese *nouveaux riches* want to display their new-found wealth in order to prove their worth. These are obviously still a very small minority in the population of 1.3 billion, although their numbers in absolute terms are quite stunning. Many of them have attracted the anger of others. Yet they apparently take heart at others' anger, as if such anger were synonymous with envy, and other people's envy was the telling sign of their success. This kind of thinking is not unique to the Chinese. Kenneth Galbraith in *The Affluent Society* (1958) had already depicted the tendency of Americans to spend and spend, in order to 'keep up with the Joneses', not in order to satisfy any 'true needs'. A more recent book by de Graaf *et al.* (2002) described the same phenomenon, and the authors aptly called it 'affluenza', to underscore that the mentality is contagious like a disease. In recent years I came across the term gigayacht for the first time, and discovered that this is the name of the game for the super-rich, who like to measure their success by the size and luxury content of their boats. This is how a CNN story described the nature of gigayachts[1]:

> for the billionaire who has everything, sometimes a superyacht just isn't enough—that's why the world's wealthiest are buying 'gigayachts.'
>
> These boats are the ultimate status symbol—a sign of eminence, power and a seemingly limitless supply of cash. And when it comes to showing off wealth and status it seems the rule is 'the bigger the better'.
>
> 'There's definitely a "mine is bigger than yours" syndrome in this industry and there is a desire to have the best. That's the great thing about these yachts,' said Jonathan Beckett, CEO of Burgess Yachts, one of the world's leading yacht brokers.

It is interesting to note why some people need to spend so much in order to feel dignified, while others do not have the same need. To put it differently, some people can achieve the mental good of feeling dignified with very little resource, while some can achieve the same mental good only with huge demand on the earth's scarce resources. Indeed, some people feel dignified and particularly proud of leaving only a very small ecological footprint on earth, while others feel dignified only by consuming hundreds or even thousands of times what an average human being on this planet consumes. Yet as far as mental goods are concerned extravagant people do not really enjoy more. While they do enjoy more of the physical goods they have long gone past the point of physical satiation. This is the key to understanding the Easterlin (1974) paradox, namely that while higher incomes apparently bring more happiness (up to a point) in cross-section studies, economic growth, which results in higher per capita incomes over the long term, does not appear to make people happier.

Inefficient household production

When I first learnt economics, I was confronted with the proposition of 'non-satiation' that was taken to be true. 'Resources are limited, but human wants are unlimited, so human beings have to confront the "economic problem" of scarcity.' The youthful mind in me wanted to challenge this view, and I came up with a concept of 'relative satiation': 'in a given period of time, for any given good, there must be a physical limit to how much we consume to reach satiation, so relative satiation can be defined as a percentage, much like relative humidity is defined'. But then I was told: 'People may keep demanding better quality, and there is no end to the quality that people demand.'

A recent book came out directly challenging the concept of non-satiation. In the introduction of *How Much is Enough: Money and the Good Life*, Skidelsky and Skidelsky wrote:

> The premise of what follows is that the material conditions of the good life already exist, at least in the affluent parts of the world, but that the blind pursuit of growth puts it continually out of reach. Under such circumstances, the aim of policy and other forms of collective actions should be to secure an economic organization that places the good things of life – health, respect, friendship, leisure and so on – within reach of all. Economic growth should be accepted as a residual, not something to be aimed at.

The phrase 'blind pursuit of growth' begs the question: why do people pursue growth blindly, and not for the good life? Why is there a rat race rather than a genuine pursuit of the good life?

After many years of reflecting on this question I finally got the answer, when I came up with the concept of mental goods. People do not live on bread alone. There are things that money cannot buy.[2] They also want pride, recognition, sense of success, love, peace, sense of security, freedom from fear and autonomy. Many of the material goods that people buy are really aimed at filling our mental good needs, and not physical needs. People spend huge amounts of money on luxury goods, in particular, not so much because of the additional physical comfort or enjoyment derived from them but largely because they then can procure a sense of success, of superiority, of recognition. They join the rat race because they want to stay ahead of others.

But some people have freed themselves from the rat race, and they feel great success and joy, and at the same time a strong sense of being in command and at ease with themselves, without having to commit so much of our resources.

Using the language of economics, we can say that those who seek greater wealth blindly have very inefficient household production functions. Remarkably, these inefficient production functions have to do with a materialistic culture. Kasser (2003) and Kasser *et.al.* (2004) explained that such materialistic culture may have to do with 'social modeling' and 'insecurity'. Social modelling, put simply, is following the example of others with whom one associates. Insecurity drives materialism because insecure people may believe that commanding more resources will offer them more security. Clearly, it is natural for people to be influenced by their peers, and there is nothing wrong with desiring a greater sense of security. But once acculturated to materialistic thinking, people tend to lose their sense of judgement. They tend to give up their ethical sense when it gets in their way as they seek greater wealth.

A recent and quite a notable study by Piff *et.al.* (2012), published in *Proceedings of the National Academy of Sciences*, found that rich people tend to be more tolerant of unethical behaviour. The study consists of carefully designed experiments and observations of behaviour in real life involving people from different backgrounds as test subjects.

One experiment recruited 195 adults using Craigslist to play a game in which a computer was supposed to roll dice for the chance of winning a $50 gift certificate. The numbers each participant rolled were actually the same without the participants knowing it; anyone self-reporting a total higher than 12 was lying about their score. Those in wealthier groups were found to be three times as likely to lie as others.[3]

Another test asked 108 adults found through a work-recruiting website of Amazon.com to assume the role of an employer negotiating a salary with job seekers. They were told several things about the job, including that it was temporary. Upper-class individuals were found less likely to disclose the temporary nature of the job.

Still another set of tests, which involved 426 cars, found that wealthier people tended to be less concerned about others' safety. First, about one-third of drivers in expensive cars were found to cut off other drivers at an intersection watched by the researchers, about double those in cheaper cars. Second, almost half of the more expensive cars did not yield when a pedestrian entered the crosswalk while all of the lowest-status cars did.

According to the authors, this could reflect 'a set of *culturally shared norms* among upper class individuals'. In particular, their wealth and status may make them more independent and may disconnect them from others and make them less sensitive to the other people's wellbeing. 'It really shows the extreme lengths to which wealth and upper-rank status in society can shape patterns of self-interest and unethicality', Paul Piff of UC Berkeley was reported to have remarked.[4]

An interesting question is: what drives the unethical behaviour? An earlier study suggests that envy could be at work. Gino and Pierce (2009) reported how subjects working under an honour system to pay themselves according to the number of correct answers in an anagram task behaved differently when they were presented with the sight of two different piles of cash from which the payout was to be made. They found that participants were far more likely to overstate their performance when they had seen the bigger pile of cash than when they had seen the smaller pile. This suggests that people may be tempted to become unethical at the sight of a big pile of cash. Another experiment included questions assessing the propensity for envious feelings under different situations. The authors found that those who were more prone to envy and who saw the big cash pile cheated more, suggesting that envious people were stimulated to cheat by the sight of the big cash pile. A third test showed that the overstatement score, defined as the fraction of times the participant overstated productivity relative to the number of times he/she missed the goal, was higher in the wealthy condition than in the poor condition, with the overstatement score at 0.56 versus 0.14 in the poor condition. Moreover, the average number of overstated rounds was higher in the wealthy condition at 3.33, as compared with only 1.79 in the case of the poor condition. This difference is statistically highly significant.

It seems that the 'culturally shared norms' of the rich in part may have something to do with the fact that they are rich, in part with the greater diversity of wealth among the rich, and in part with certain ways and practices that are common to the business world in which they happen to live. If they are much richer than others, their lives become more and more detached from those of the others. At the same time, within the relatively small circle of the rich, diversity of wealth is much bigger than that within the circle of ordinary working-class people. As the relative rise or fall may be quite rapid within this group the pressure to keep up with one's peers is quite intense among the rich, while among the circle of ordinary working-class people, getting ahead or falling is not such a big deal, because the number of ordinary folks is huge, and the relative rise or decline within this ocean of ordinary folks is often not even noticeable. Finally, in the business world where exchange of favours is often taken as good for mutual benefits, it is easy to develop an increasing tolerance of corrupt practices.

It would of course be wrong to think of rich people as all sharing similar norms and values. Warren Buffett is so vastly different from Donald Trump, for instance. One is low-key and does not care much for a luxurious life; the other is all for glamour and high life. A good question is: what makes them so different?

Actually Warren Buffett and Donald Trump, as well as you and me, are the same in that each of us tends to make reference to a group as our peers. In general, everyone has a strong desire not to fall behind one's peers in the dimensions considered important by these peers. Besides, everyone has an inclination to act in a way that is regarded as acceptable by people in the reference group. Warren Buffett and Donald Trump are different in large part because they make reference to different people as their peers. Very often, this makes all the difference in the formation of culturally shared norms, and here, crucially, choice comes in. As much as 'affluenza' is contagious, some people can get immunised, largely through the formation of values and models for emulation, and then even though they are quite affluent, they may not share the same norms as the others who contract the 'affluenza virus'.

Efficient household production

There is thus such a thing as acculturisation. If we socialise and associate with people who are ethical, who believe in conservation, who love nature more than the high life, we tend to adopt similar values, because that is how we gain recognition by those we are associated with. Then the 'production' of crucially needed mental goods through various household activities will become much more efficient. In a fundamental sense people acculturated to a simpler, less extravagant lifestyle are no less happy than those who leave a very costly ecological footprint every day of their lives, because like them they are able to achieve the respect and recognition of those that they associate with. In Figure 3.1, just because the household socialises and identifies with people who prefer to leave a small ecological footprint in their activities, the 'household production function' has become different. Less input is required, and yet the mental goods aren't that much different from those in Figure 3.2.

One may, of course, query the definition of luxury goods and non-luxury goods. We know that many of the goods that were considered luxury goods today may not be considered luxury goods at all. Air conditioners, television (particularly colour television) and refrigerators are today considered necessities in many places. In the present context, however, luxury goods refer specifically to goods that are acquired specifically to show off one's wealth and status, and

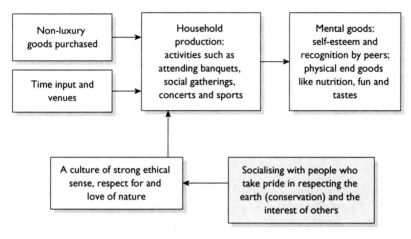

Figure 3.1 Efficient household production.

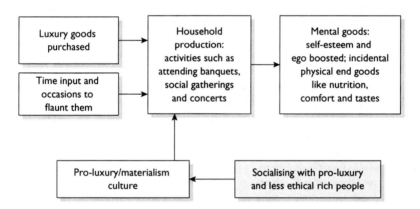

Figure 3.2 Inefficient household production.

so they are synonymous with conspicuous consumption. Conspicuous consumption is intended clearly not just for the physical benefit of the actual goods, but, more importantly, for the benefit of the mental good derived – the thought that one is somehow better placed than others in wealth or in lifestyle. Professor Yew-Kwang Ng (1987) coined the term 'diamond good' to refer to goods that offer consumers utility beyond the utility from the physical qualities of the goods, in particular utility based on the knowledge that the good is scarce and costly – sufficient to put their owners in a class distinct from others.

While 'diamond goods' and conspicuous consumption in general certainly contribute to utility, and rich people certainly can afford and normally do consume more luxury items, a huge literature now suggests that incomes above a certain level may not bring much additional happiness at all. Recent examples include Kahneman and Deaton (2010), and Easterlin *et.al.* (2010)[5] Kahneman and Deaton noted that 'when plotted against log income, life evaluation rises steadily. Emotional well-being also rises with log income, but there is no further progress beyond an annual income of $75,000'. Life evaluation is a measure of 'total life satisfaction' with respondents evaluating their current life on the Cantril Self-Anchoring Scale, in which 0 is 'the worst possible life for you' and 10 is 'the best possible life for you'. Given the way 'satisfaction' is normally understood, the respondent is likely to interpret more in terms of material wellbeing and then only secondarily in terms of mental goods. As such it is no wonder that higher income leads to a higher rating. But Kahneman and Deaton's plotting of positive affect, 'stress-free', and 'not blue' (i.e. not sad nor worrying), against income shows that these dimensions of wellbeing clearly level off roughly around an annual income of around $75,000. These aspects of 'emotional wellbeing' reflect mental goods, and suggest that people with very high incomes do not enjoy mental goods any better than people with an 'adequate income', which would have amounted to approximately $75,000 in the United States in 2010.

Easterlin and his coauthors (2010) found that the 'happiness–income paradox' not only holds for developed countries, which was the earlier finding, but also for developing countries and such transitioning economies as the eastern European countries that were previously socialist planned economies as well, if one looks at data over 10 years and beyond. In particular, while China doubled its real per capita income in less than 10 years, and South Korea and Chile in 13 and 18 years respectively, 'one might think many of the people in these countries would be so happy, they'd be dancing in the streets'. But Easterlin and his coauthors were surprised to find nothing like that. Although these countries have made big advances in procuring the physical goods for their compatriots, apparently they have been extraordinarily – or not so extraordinarily – unsuccessful in improving the lots of their compatriots in terms of advancing 'emotional wellbeing' through procuring the mental goods that their compatriots aspire for. Keeping up with the Joneses somehow produces only a fleeting increase in utility, an increase that evaporates into thin air in no time, because not everyone can be ahead of others.

Conclusions

Culture plays a key role in the efficiency of household activities in generating the mental goods that all people need in order to live a happy life, and culture is related to the decisions, often made without our awareness or careful deliberation, as to whom we associate and socialise with. Once we have identified whom we regard as our peers, we seek their acceptance and recognition by trying to perform according to the standards and value system of this peer group. If our identified peers all value a luxurious life, we will need to live a luxurious life in order to achieve self-esteem and perceived recognition by our peers. Household production of the mental good 'self-esteem' will then become very costly. On the other hand, if our identified peers all value a simple life, we will not need to spend much, and yet we will still enjoy the mental good.

This analysis extends to those people who are spiritually inspired,[6] and who, instead of identifying with people who live around them, identify with certain spiritual teachers who may even be historical figures or legendary spiritual teachers. Their self-esteem then is based on the standards set by their spiritual teachers. When they feel that they are abiding by those standards, they will enjoy the self-esteem and inner peace that others may find difficult to apprehend. This is so notwithstanding, or because they lead a simple life (Kasser, 2009).

As we will see in the next chapter, culture is an aspect of *mental capital*, and mental capital can be positive or negative. We can invest in positive 'mental capital' that dramatically increases the efficiency of the production function and should avoid building up negative mental capital.

Notes

1 edition.cnn.com/2011/09/13/travel/rise-gigayacht/index.html.
2 *What Money Can't Buy* is the title of a best seller by Michael F. Sandel, published by Farrar, Straus and Giroux, 2012.
3 A reviewer of this book suggests that ruthlessness may be positively associated with wealth, so the causality could be the other way round. That is to say, because some people are ruthless and unethical, they could amass a fortune.
4 ABC Newcastle, Australia, February 28, 2012: www.abc.net.au/news/2012-02-28/upper-class-people-more-likely-to-cheat-says-study/3856172/default.htm?site=newcastle; www.bloomberg.com/news/2012-02-27/wealthier-people-more-likely-than-poorer-to-lie-or-cheat-researchers-find.html.
5 www.pnas.org/content/107/52/22463.abstract?sid=6699db95-04ed-45af-8450-074fe609aa6f.
6 It is necessary to distinguish between religious and spiritual. Some people are religious in the sense of following religious routines strictly but they may not be spiritual. Being religious is not a necessary precondition to being spiritual.

Chapter 4

Mental capital and habit formation, with a digression to spiritual capital

Introduction

Psychologists talk about *psychological capital*. It refers to four qualities that serve as an asset to individuals, allowing them to overcome difficulties and achieve better outcomes. These include *self-efficacy, optimism, hope* and *resiliency* (Luthans and Youssef, 2004). Self-efficacy is a feeling of being in control of oneself and able to meet the challenges of the moment. Optimism is a belief that any negative factor is likely to be temporary and specific to a situation while the positive factors are permanent and more general. Hope is 'having the will power and the pathways to attain one's goals'. Resilience is the ability to tough it out through adversity and to bounce back from disappointments and failures. These qualities are seen to contribute to better work performance and psychological health.

In this chapter, I shall discuss an alternative, though related, concept, called *mental capital*, which is more akin to the concept of *capital* as used in economics. Economists define *capital* as a produced means of production. Thus firms invest to acquire the machinery and equipment and buildings to help them produce, while individuals acquire human capital to become more productive and competitive in the job market. *Investing* is accumulating capital. The services of capital assets form a 'factor of production' or an input used in the production of outputs. So mental capital is the mental capability of an individual that accumulates over the years and that contributes to production, which may be in a commercial or household setting.

When the mental capital is in the form of skills and a capacity that contribute to commercial/economic production it is called *human capital*, and the pertinent skills can be called *jobs skills*. When the mental capital is in the form of skills and a capacity that contribute to household production, it can be called *life capital*, and the pertinent skills can be called *life skills*. Two of the most important life skills are *reflective skills* and *learning skills*, which are related and which will be further discussed below. Life capital is manifested by four qualities: Love, Insight, Fortitude, and Engagement.

In household production the end goods include physical end goods like (nutrition and taste from) dinners and movies enjoyed at home, and mental

Mental capital and habit formation 33

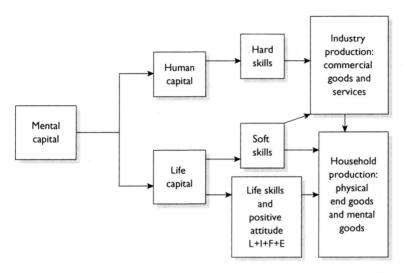

Figure 4.1 Mental capital.

goods like having good company, a sense of autonomy, self-efficacy, confidence, self-esteem, composure, sense of success and sense of self-actualisation. As such, mental capital certainly encompasses the four elements of psychological capital named by psychologists, but it includes much more (Figure 4.1).

Figure 4.2 shows that *mental capital can potentially grow into spiritual capital*. As an individual gains more mental capital and benefits from it, a wish that the same benefit can be enjoyed by others may grow. As this wish grows, the individual gradually broadens his perspective, eventually transcending himself, and develops a compassion for all others. Forgetting himself, he simply goes about doing everything that needs to be done and within his capacity. In so doing he

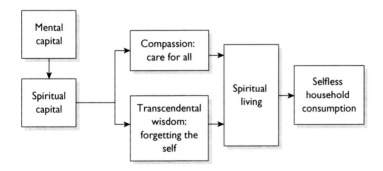

Figure 4.2 Spiritual capital.

maximises the welfare for humanity to the best of his ability without thinking about himself. Even as he eats and drinks to maintain his survival and keeps his health, he does that because that is his duty. Again, using the Kantian terminology, the *categorical imperative* is to serve humanity selflessly.

The concept of spiritual capital has attracted research from mainstream economists and other social scientists. According to the John Templeton Foundation[1]:

> This research recognizes how social and economic dynamics are shaped by cultural factors ... The specific term 'spiritual capital' refers to that aspect of social capital linked with religion and/or spirituality. In the last ten years, Robert Fogel (University of Chicago and 1993 Nobel Laureate in Economics) and others have explored and used the term. In one sense, then, spiritual capital might be seen as a significant subset of social capital. According to Robert Putnam's influential work on social capital, religion is by far the largest generator of social capital in the United States, contributing to more than half of the social capital in the country.

Ho (2012) distinguished *social spiritual capital* from an individual's spiritual capital.

> Social spiritual capital does not refer to the number of churches, mosques, temples, and other worshipping places that can be found in a country. Social spiritual capital refers, rather, to the interconnectedness of the human existence that awakens each individual to the common roots of humanity (p. 47).

An individual's spiritual capital, on the other hand, refers to an individual's capacity to think beyond himself and even to forget himself, simply devoting his life to making life a bounty rather than a burden for everyone. Fully developed spiritual people do this as part of their nature, because they have transcended the ego into human beings beyond their physical being[2] (Figure 4.2).

Formation of habits

As we live, the thoughts and activities which we go through each day have an impact on us. As we keep repeating certain ways of thinking, speaking, or behaviour, we form habits, and as habits form, our responses to stimuli become automatic, and gradually out of our conscious control. We effectively program ourselves to respond to certain tasks or responses in the way we are used to. These automatic or even reflexive responses can be good for us or bad for us. Without these automatic or reflexive responses, musicians cannot possibly play their music. It would then be virtually impossible for performers to play out their pieces and be able to express their emotions. There is simply no time to think between one note and the next note, or one group of notes and the next group of notes. The training of the musical performer consists of many years of repetitive training that in the end makes music making almost automatic. Musical sense and musical playing skills are a form of mental capital.

On the other hand, there are reflexive and habitual responses that may be bad – not because moralists call them bad but because they end up undermining the wellbeing of the individuals. For example, as children grow up living in an environment in which they are criticised in an unfriendly manner that makes them hate to be criticised, their *self-defence mechanism* may build up so that they automatically reject even friendly criticisms and spontaneously give excuses when anything goes wrong. This would prevent them from learning from their mistakes. Other bad habits include procrastination, not fastening the seatbelt in cars, losing our temper at irritations, and carelessness. Some may disagree that losing our temper is a habit. But it is indeed a habit, meaning that people can often train themselves not to lose their temper.

Ann Graybiel, Walter A. Rosenblith professor of neuroscience in MIT's Department of Brain and Cognitive Sciences, saw some physiological reasons behind why bad habits were hard to break. She noted that, when habits are formed, often through repetitive behaviour in certain contexts that offer specific stimulations, such as smoking and gambling, neural activity patterns in a specific region of the brain are changed. 'It is as though, somehow, the brain retains a memory of the habit context, and this pattern can be triggered if the right habit cues come back.' As much as we may like to kick a habit, the sight of a trigger, such as the sight of a piece of chocolate for someone who wants to control their weight, could ruin all previous effort.[3] When a bad habit is formed, it becomes a *negative mental capital* that keeps undermining our wellbeing, because we would then effectively lose control of ourselves, and succumb to the potentially ruinous inertia that prevents us from reaching greater goals that await us.

On the other hand, when good habits are formed, they keep benefiting us, and they become part of our (positive) mental capital. This mental capital benefits us in several ways:

- We will be able to draw on it when we need it, and the reflexes that we have acquired allow us to do things that we otherwise cannot accomplish, so we gain self-efficacy.
- As we gain more mental capital, we also gain more confidence, which is a mental good. Confidence allows us to realise our potential.
- An important aspect of mental capital is the promise of a better future, which we will reckon is within our reach. So we gain hope and optimism.
- We also gain resilience in due course. Since learning from a mistake has become a habit, we reckon that mistakes and failures contribute to our growth. Instead of being beaten by the failure or hurt by the mistake, we will learn, and gain more mental capital stock. This contributes to a virtuous circle of learning and growth.

Charles Duhigg, in his best seller (*The Power of Habit: Why We Do What We Do in Life and Business*), published in 2012, recounts dozens of real stories of people transforming their lives from chaos to order, from flop to success, from lack of direction to meaningful and fruitful pursuits. And every time the miracle happened because the person at a crucial point in life decided to change one of his or her old habits and focused his or her mind on it. As Duhigg so ably demonstrates, entire organisations and even societies can be transformed when habits change. Like Graybiel, Duhigg pointed out that changes in habits ultimately lead to physical changes in the brain, which at once informs us of the daunting task of breaking an old bad habit and the desirability of forming new good habits.

If Duhigg convinces you about the importance of habit formation, James Claiborn and Cherry Pedrick (2001) and Travis Bradberry and Jean Greaves (2009) offer clues as to how to break old habits, most importantly by raising our self-awareness, or *mindfulness* – realizing that we are slipping back to the old habits whenever we do so, and by constant self-reminders about the desirability of the goal that we have set for ourselves. Writing a daily journal about our own failures or successes at handling our habits is just a strategy of raising and reinforcing such awareness.

Mental capital, comprising an accumulation of habits that are truly useful and good for us, and emptying out habits that are harmful for us, is then the source and basis of self-efficacy, optimism, hope and resilience – the psychological capital that psychologists talk about.

Reflecting, imitating, drilling and learning

Human behaviour is mostly driven by desires and *motivations*. This means that there are certain goals that people want to achieve, and then they go about trying to achieve them. Sometimes these goals may not even be obvious to the person, as the person pursues such goals instinctively. Sometimes they are clearer, and the individual deliberates to achieve them. When individuals succeed in achieving those goals they reckon that they have done the right thing, and tend to take the same strategy or act the same way the next time they want to achieve their goal. A crucial question is: what will they do if they fail?

There are two diametrically different responses to a failure. One that is very common is to be upset, and in frustration let out the anger that may be waiting to be released. This anger could be very destructive. It could hurt people close to us, and damage relations between them and us. If those near to us are themselves emotionally not very stable or vulnerable, serious consequences could occur. Along with the anger is another natural response: blaming others or the circumstances for preventing the achievement of our goals. In focusing on the blame game, we lose sight of the mistakes that we may have made, and the opportunity for self-correction. Once we have developed a habit of getting angry and blaming this and that for our failures, a negative capital forms, and then it will be very difficult to break away from this. People can fall into a very miserable life.

On the other hand, we could conduct a careful and systematic assessment of why we failed. This is called *reflection*. Realising what was not done right and what may be done better is called *learning*. *Learning by doing* is understanding failures and mistakes and overcoming them one by one so that avoidable mistakes can be prevented in the future. Good reflective skills would involve an objective, systematic assessment of the circumstances and the reasons for the failure, and considering what may be done to enhance the chances of success next time. Perhaps we may not have been well enough prepared; perhaps we may have missed out telling signs that would have warned us not to do what we did; perhaps we should have been better organised, and so on and so forth.

One can never guarantee success the next time. Often there will be uncontrollable factors that cannot be anticipated in advance. But with reflection and learning, the chances for success next time will be that much higher. More importantly, even if we still fail to do it, the reflection and learning imply that we are 'growing up', and not just 'growing old'. 'Growing up' is itself a great success, and makes our lives that much more meaningful and fun.

In a sense learning is the gradual formation of an appropriate reflex to a situation. For some people, reflecting becomes a habit. Whenever they have gone through a new experience, they automatically look back to assess what they have done right and what and how they could have done better. The habit of reflection is a tremendous mental capital.

Learning a musical instrument or a new language is obviously the acquisition of new reflexes. In learning a language, for example, simply understanding how a foreign language works and the grammar will not allow you to use it. To use a new language requires a reflexive or almost reflexive response whenever it has to be used. There is no time to think through the sentence structure and the vocabulary. All that needs to be spoken must be spoken spontaneously. When a new language habit is formed, the mental capital will be enhanced. To acquire a new language, considerable drilling is required, consciously or unconsciously. The same applies to learning a musical instrument. Without acquiring the needed reflexes, and just relying on logic and understanding, it is like learning to swim onshore. It will never work.

Usually it takes a lot of effort, and it needs motivation. For adults who clearly know what they want, the motivation will be there, but then they could easily succumb to laziness or the curse of 'not having enough time', which often reflects a habit of making an excuse, though sometimes may be genuine. Overcoming excuses is a big challenge that promises personal growth.

For children who may not know what they want, often it is the parents who want them to learn something. Sometimes parents like to offer material rewards as a lure to motivate. But psychologists have long found that material rewards may not be very effective, and they certainly are not reliable. They can only motivate for some time, but they seldom become an engine that keeps giving the child the energy and enthusiasm to learn. The greatest motivation for children is always when they themselves see the goals are desirable. The next most important motivation for children is when the learning process itself becomes fun or at least not a punishing experience. Too many parents make a learning experience a punishing experience. As a result they destroy any incentive for kids to learn.

Imagine a child starting to learn a new task but who is not good at it. The parent is frustrated and yells at the child, and keeps saying he is not doing it right, and demands that he do better. That is a punishing experience that the child will never forget. It will haunt him for a long time. Learning is quickly associated with the punishing experience, and it is quite natural that he will lose enthusiasm and interest.

On the other hand, when a child is not doing so well, the parent expresses appreciation for the child's effort, and tells him that he is already pretty good as a beginner, and that he shows great promise at being quite good at it before long. The child is likely to be motivated.

To reiterate: although learning requires understanding, it also often involves habit formation and is sometimes a change of old habits. Reflection is an important element in learning; imitating and repetitive 'drilling' are an important pathway to the formation of the needed habits. Appropriate reflexive responses in context are the hallmark of successful learning.

Habits and the genius within

There is another sense in which habits can become a negative mental capital or a positive mental capital. When we have become so used to a way of thinking that we automatically forget the possibility of an alternative we will have lost the possibility of creativity. When we are so used to our personal experience we may simply rule out the possibility of anything that is out of this experience. Before human beings ever flew, flying was considered impossible. Humanity had to wait until 1903 when the Wright brothers invented, built and successfully tested the world's first airborne vehicle. Before the telephone was invented, no one took Alexander Bell seriously when he claimed he could make a gadget that would allow people to converse over a longer distance than the human voice could naturally travel. We could easily assume we could not do this, and even ridicule the inventor for being silly. Actually we have been conditioned by our limited experience and our lack of an open mind.

Breaking from a way of thinking that has become a habit is sometimes just what it takes to become a genius. We cannot live without reflexes. But we must not be confined by our reflexes. We are so used to logical and linear thinking – step-by-step arguments and derivations – that we automatically follow such lines of thinking, but thinking 'out of the box' is needed to break new ground. This is sometimes called lateral thinking.[4]

Conclusions

Mental capital, consisting of good habits and good reflexes, benefits our lives and allows us to achieve our dreams. But there is also negative mental capital in the form of bad habits that undermine our dreams. The habits and reflexes are good or bad not because a moralist tells us they are good or bad, but because they benefit or harm our longer-term interest.

Interestingly, as we accumulate more and more positive mental capital we automatically gain confidence in ourselves and enjoy a sense of autonomy, and become immensely happier. With a strong stock of mental capital, we are at ease, because we know that we have become masters of ourselves. We will have gained self-efficacy, optimism, hope and resilience, which constitute what psychologists call 'psychological capital'. We will be better able to do what we want, be less affected by anxiety and stress, and we will know our limits and avoid creating excessive pressures for ourselves. The world suddenly has become wonderful!

Notes

1 capabilities.templeton.org/2004/horiz03.html, accessed 11 April 2012.
2 See Ho (2011a) for a fuller discussion of human spirituality.
3 web.mit.edu/newsoffice/2005/habit.html.
4 See De Bono (1970).

Chapter 5

The happiness formula

Introduction: what is happiness?

A really fundamental question is: what is happiness? While this could provoke deep philosophical investigation, for our purposes the answer is very simple: happiness is subjective wellbeing. As such, a person's happiness is not for anyone else to define except the person himself or herself, whose personal experience for good or for ill is the litmus test for its validity. Still, we need to distinguish between a moment's joy or excitement and a more 'enduring level of happiness,' which was the subject of discussion in Seligman's book *Authentic Happiness* (2003). It is exactly such an enduring level of happiness that we seek to promote.

Martin Seligman, widely considered the father of positive psychology, asked us to consider the equation

$$H = S + C + V$$

According to Seligman, H is 'the enduring level of happiness', S is 'your set range', C is 'the circumstances of your life' And V represents 'factors under your voluntary control'.

The 'enduring level of happiness' is not just about the happiness 'these days'. Unfortunately this is the way the key happiness question is often asked in many questionnaires in happiness studies.[1] The enduring level of happiness is certainly not the same as the mood of the moment; neither is it the 'utility' derived from an experience or from an episode in life. The enduring level of happiness is 'taking everything together, and looking at your life as a whole, how happy or unhappy you are'.

This *enduring level of happiness* by definition is not expected to change from moment to moment, even though one's assessment of it may still vary somewhat from time to time, and measurement error could exist as the respondent perceives the question differently from how it is intended. Moreover, these assessments will unavoidably be influenced by situational factors. Still, in asking a person to assess him life as a whole, you are inviting him to take a holistic view of his life. Understood this way, it is not surprising that people's reports of subjective wellbeing would fluctuate around this enduring level of happiness. Accordingly, I would amend the interpretation of that equation, and propose that S, or the 'set range', mirrors the real enduring level of happiness. H is, instead, only the reported happiness score, even though the respondent may be asked to give a score on overall happiness.

Actually I would propose an amendment to this formula. Instead of H being equal to $S + C + V$, it is postulated that S depends on both genetic factors and voluntary control. Mathematically, we can write:

$$H = S(G, V) + C(t, V)$$

which simply says that the set point of happiness is in part genetically determined, and in part behaviourally determined, while situational happiness, representing a deviation from the set point, will vary (vanish) with time, and will also be partly affected by behaviour. Certainly our temperament and personality are in part shaped by what we choose to do[2]; certainly circumstances are in part determined by how we conduct our life and make our decisions.

In a sense, the enduring level of happiness is generally not the same as 'total life satisfaction'. Given the imprecision of language, in responding to a question on 'total life satisfaction' respondents will likely assess if there is something in their life that they would consider not totally satisfactory. A blind person certainly would prefer that he could have his eyesight restored. Inevitably anyone will not be fully satisfied with everything. As mortals we make mistakes and we cannot be totally satisfied with everything that we have done. Yet a blind person can be 'perfectly happy', not in the sense of being in 'perfect bliss' but in the sense of being genuinely happy. A parent with a mentally handicapped child cannot be 'totally satisfied', and yet again he or she can be 'perfectly happy'. I have even heard a parent with a mentally handicapped child saying the child is a great gift from God. This parent might score a 9 or even 10 for happiness (on a scale of 0–10), but most probably would report a lower score on total life satisfaction.

What is set range?

Seligman used the term set range, suggesting that even the genetically determined level of happiness may vary over a range randomly.

Our blood pressure may go up or down with changes in activities and changes in the level of intensity of these activities. But it will return to the normal range, which in a sense is intrinsic and biologically determined.

Similarly the 'set range', according to its proponents, refers to a range of happiness that we are born with. It is a range because it may not be a definite value and may cover a range of values. It is believed to be 'set' by biological factors that will determine the personal traits or personality which ultimately affect our subjective wellbeing of what happens to us.[3] According to Martin Seligman, we could work to lift up our happiness, but 'The best you can do with positive emotion is you can get people to live at the top of their set range.'[4] It is held that we could deviate from the set range from time to time, as happy events or unhappy events take place, but we would return to the set range in due course.

It is a fact that happy or unhappy events normally do not leave much mark on a person's reported happiness: they 'are largely gone after just 3 months and undetectable after 6 months'.[5] Lykken made a remarkable observation about subjective wellbeing (SWB):

> One can predict a person's SWB far more accurately from his identical cotwin's score even ten years earlier than from that person's income, professional status, or social position today. Those favored genetically by high IQs are indeed more likely to become doctors, lawyers, or chieftains of industry than are those destined to be plumbers or garbage collectors—but those clever ones are not likely to end up any happier.

But it would be wrong to draw the conclusion from this observation that there is little one can do to change happiness permanently. While agreeing that there is indeed a set range to which one's reported subjective wellbeing tends to return, I hypothesise that this set range is really determined by a person's *mental capital*, and while mental capital cannot change overnight, it is not immutable either. With early intervention, patience, will and perseverance, negative mental capital can gradually be reduced; positive mental capital can accumulate. A person's mental capital may in part be determined genetically, in the sense that some people tend to be more stubborn and more reserved while others may be more open-minded and outward-looking, and that these traits may be inherited. Nevertheless people can change their mental capital, *by working sufficiently hard, appropriately, and over a sufficiently long stretch of time consistently.* Some people may need to work harder to accumulate their mental capital; others may acquire it more easily. Although some people need to make a greater effort to be happy, they need not be less happy than others once they have accumulated the requisite mental capital.

C and V

Seligman notes that circumstances may affect a person's reported SWB. But all of the circumstances that may make a person happier are subject to limitations and their effects are at best very transient. While extreme poverty makes a person unhappy, and a higher income will make him happier, it is now recognised that there is a limit to which higher income will bring more happiness, as was discussed by Kahneman and Deaton and others. It is also proven that, while winning a lottery generally makes one happy for some time, for most people with a moderate to good income the positive effects will disappear altogether in no more than 6 months. While disabling illness could produce a more enduring effect on happiness and life satisfaction, unless there are 'five or more [health] problems', Seligman noted that the negative effect is 'not nearly as much as you might expect'. My own observation is that people with enduring pain can indeed be very unhappy, but people with a disability (such as blindness, loss of the use of a limb or deafness) need not be unhappy at all. Enduring and severe pain invariably makes people very miserable, because it cannot be easily dismissed or forgotten. But there are many examples of people overcoming even severe disabilities cheerfully.

V, the voluntary factor, is really the crucial one, and it is the attitude of the person that allows him to overcome disabilities and remain cheerful. Using the language we used before, V consists of the effort to accumulate positive mental capital and to reduce negative mental capital. Many experiments, involving subjects going through appropriate training sessions, have proven that a positive attitude can be acquired, and that is the *raison d'être* of positive psychology.

It is important to recognise that there are things within our control and things that are outside our control. Things that are within our control are 'decision variables'. Things that are outside our control are 'constraints'. Recognising the true constraints and focusing on the decision variables allows us to do the best with what we have in our lives. This is the essence of the economics of life.

It is futile to grumble or complain or dwell on the real constraints. That would be just a waste of time, and would certainly undermine our happiness.

On the other hand, some initially perceived constraints can be overcome, and then they are not real constraints. Distinguishing between the real constraints and the false ones is an important challenge, and does require constant honest reflection. Unfortunately, for some people, the idea never occurs to them that some constraints are real and that the best strategy then is to take them as given. Similarly, with some people it never occurs to them that some constraints are unreal and that they can be overcome provided that they approach the problem wisely and make a sufficient and enduring effort.

The key strategy under V is using the happiness formula in our day-to-day life, and that is LIFE – a genuine respect for and faith in life, comprising Love, Insight, Fortitude and Engagement. This four-pronged approach to lifting our enduring level of happiness is based on a vast literature in psychology, philosophy and religion, and is not my invention. In stipulating LIFE as the happiness formula, I merely bring these ideas together in an easy-to-remember formula.

Love

I have already cited Fromm's *The Art of Loving* (1956). Among religions Christianity explicitly espouses 'Love thy neighbour as thyself,' and Buddhism explicitly preaches 'compassion'. Confucianism, the main school of philosophy in traditional Chinese society, asks us to put ourselves in the shoes of others.

Insight

Insight or wisdom includes several elements. One is a sense of proportion or a sense of balance, of which work–life balance is an example. Bertrand Russell has referred to this in *The Conquest of Happiness* (1996). One is a culture or living style that effectively allows 'efficient production of mental goods'. For example, many people have learnt to achieve a sense of dignity without conspicuous consumption. Explicit reference to 'thrift' or 'avoiding excesses' is made in the philosophical classic, the *Daodejing*. Still another aspect about Insight is humility. Here is an excerpt from the *Daodejing* (Chapter 67)[6]:

> I have three treasures that I keep and adhere to always.
> The first is compassion.
> The second is thrift.
> The third is humility.

In the psychological literature much research has been done on the distinction between extrinsic and intrinsic motives and how different motivations affect happiness (Kasser and Ryan, 1993, 1996, 2001; Schmuck *et al.*, 2000; Schmuck, 2001). A common conclusion is that overemphasis on materialistic or extrinsic goals tends to lead to unhappiness.

Yet another aspect of Insight is an ability to distinguish between means and ends. The *Daodejing* reminds us that life is really the most important of all; everything else (such as money and material goods) is only a means to serving the purposes of life:

> All things under heaven with their diversity
> shall fall back to their proper places and
> shall rediscover their origins.
> Going back to one's origin is the same as stilling the mind.
> It can also be known as the Rediscovery of Life.
> The Life Rediscovered is the Eternal.
> Knowing the Eternal is true understanding.

Fortitude

Fortitude is just another word for resilience, again a subject in psychology with a vast literature.

Engagement

Engagement as purposive and active living and again has been widely discussed in the psychological literature, and is a central theme in Zen (or Chan) Buddhism. Martin Seligman has explicitly emphasised engaged living as a key to happiness, along with the pleasant life and the meaningful life.

Consider the following and truly famous prayer of Saint Francis of Assisi, which is often considered to reflect the epitome of spirituality:

Lord, make me a channel of thy peace;
that where there is hatred, I may bring love;
that where there is wrong, I may bring the spirit of forgiveness;
that where there is discord, I may bring harmony;
that where there is error, I may bring truth;
that where there is doubt, I may bring faith;
that where there is despair, I may bring hope;
that where there are shadows, I may bring light;
that where there is sadness, I may bring joy.

Lord, grant that I may seek rather to comfort than to be comforted;
to understand, than to be understood;
to love, than to be loved.

For it is by self-forgetting that one finds.

It is by forgiving that one is forgiven.

It is by dying that one awakens to eternal life.

Amen.

Here we find that Love, Insight, Fortitude and Engagement are all highlighted: Love (where there is hatred, I may bring love; where there is sadness, I may bring joy; grant that I may seek rather . . . to love, than to be loved); Insight (where there is error, I may bring truth; grant that I may seek rather . . . to understand, than to be understood; it is by self-forgetting that one finds); Fortitude (faith, hope); Engagement (to bring harmony, to bring truth, to bring faith, to bring hope, and to love; to console, to understand, to forgive – all in active rather than passive voice, all with a clear purpose).

In short, to get the most out of life we need to nurture more Love, Insight (wisdom) and Fortitude, and to live with a sense of purpose and devotion (Engagement). This is the essence of spirituality, and in what follows, I shall present some evidence about the effectiveness of LIFE in elevating happiness.

Testing LIFE, the happiness formula, using Hong Kong data

We have talked about mental capital in the last chapter. Building up mental capital allows us to become happier, because mental capital allows us to enjoy more mental goods like love, a sense of autonomy, freedom from anxiety and self-esteem. We need to make love into a habit, insight into a habit, resilience into a habit, and purposive activity into a habit. Once we have developed these habits, we will find our lives much more fulfilling, because then each day offers a new opportunity for personal growth and self-actualisation.

Over the years I have tested and confirmed this happiness formula based on Love, Insight, Fortitude and Engagement, each of which may be considered to be a dimension of mental capital. These different aspects of mental capital are not completely distinct. For example, Fortitude may be grounded on a very strong

Love, which in turn may generate a strong sense of purpose and purposive activity that is the essence of engagement. However, Love, Insight, Fortitude and Engagement form an easy-to-remember 'quartet' and remind us that, after all, LIFE represents the basic value of all activities, and this gives good educational value. The LIFE scores are all measured on an 11-point scale (from 0 to 10) to describe the extent to which the respondent agrees with a statement.

Love is measured using responses to two questions about the respondent's propensity to care for others and feelings about others having a genuine concern for the respondent's wellbeing. Love helps generate a sense of purpose and meaning in life.

- I love and care for my family.
- I am concerned about the welfare of others in the community.

Insight is measured using responses to a set of questions about the respondent's sense of proportion and priorities, ability to distinguish between means and ends, understanding that success in life is not so much outperforming others as realising the potential within, willingness and preparedness to reflect on one's decisions and to learn. Insight thus helps generate a sense of self-efficacy and autonomy, and a sense of achievement that is not dependent on others. Two crucial questions that always appear in the surveys are asking respondents to agree or disagree with the following:

1. Success is achieving one's best within one's ability.
2. I am able to keep a good balance over work, rest, and spending time with my family.

Fortitude is measured using responses to a question regarding the respondent's ability to face adversity. Fortitude helps generate a sense of achievement and inner strength. The key question participants are asked to agree with in the surveys is:

- When I face an adverse situation, I keep doing my best to deal with it with calm.

Engagement is measured using responses to questions regarding the respondent's putting thoughts into action. An engaged person is someone who actively engages in tasks that serve his identified purposes. Engagement generates a sense of self-actualisation. The respondent is asked to assess if he agrees with the following statements:

- I always look for opportunities to realise my potential.
- I have clearly identified goals and purposes in life.

The Centre for Public Policy Studies at Lingnan University started conducting annual happiness surveys in 2005 and in 2008 began its LIFE score surveys, each time using the randomised digit dialling method, on the Hong Kong population aged 21 and above.

We averaged the scores under each category and call these LIFE scores. We discovered that reported happiness, also rated on a scale from 0 to 10, can be explained by these LIFE scores very well, and that the LIFE scores generally rise with age. The LIFE scores from 2008 to 2011 from the randomised telephone survey are presented in Table 5.1. Two striking results are apparent. First, female LIFE scores are almost always higher than those of males. Second, LIFE scores clearly tend to rise with age, with the exception of the Engagement score, which does show a decline with age. The increases in the Love, Insight, and Fortitude scores over the life cycle for both males and females are all quite consistent. This result corroborates a recent finding by Mogilner *et al.* (2011) that 'Whereas younger people are more likely to associate happiness with excitement, as they get older, they become more likely to associate happiness with peacefulness.' Older people are less focused on the joy or excitement of the moment, and tend to take a more holistic view toward life.

Table 5.2 presents the results of a statistical test with the happiness score regressed against the LIFE scores and various demographic and economic status variables. It shows that LIFE variables all carry statistically highly significant coefficients, all with the right signs, suggesting that higher LIFE scores are associated with higher happiness. Moreover, with the age group below 30 left out (to serve as the benchmark, so the coefficients reported are relative to this group), the age group coefficients show a drop in happiness for the 30–49 age group relative to the younger cohort and then an even bigger drop for the 50 and above group, which is different from the result commonly reported about a cited U-shaped happiness profile (Blanchflower and Oswald, 2007; Stone *et al.*, 2010). The different result is likely to be related to the fact that the effects of LIFE scores have been controlled in the equation, and both Love and Insight scores tend to rise with age.[7] Female still carries a positive coefficient, and so does married. Financial stress carries a significant negative coefficient. Income categories carry the expected signs, with the lowest income group least happy but the highest income group – those with HK$40,000 monthly income (around US$61,500 annual income) – not enjoying any noticeable increase in happiness. Given Hong Kong's lower tax rate and taking purchasing power parity into account, HK$40,000 monthly pre-tax income is rather similar to an annual pre-tax income of US$75,000 in the United States in real purchasing power after tax, thus corroborating Kahneman and Deaton's results.

Here again the LIFE variables all carry highly significant coefficients, and once again, the Engagement variable carries the biggest coefficient, followed by Insight, Love and Fortitude, in that order. Ageing is here seen to have a negative effect on happiness, after the LIFE variables have been controlled. It should be noted that in this sample there are more females than males, and female happiness tends to be more negatively related to age. Female and married again appear to have positive effects on happiness. Unemployment and financial stress carry the expected negative signs. In this sample, the high household monthly

Table 5.1 LIFE scores by sex and age groupings: telephone survey data from Hong Kong

Age	Sex		2008 L	I	F	E	2009 L	I	F	E	2010 L	I	F	E	2011 L	I	F	E	HI*
<50 years	Male	Mean	7.20	6.21	6.48	6.28	7.17	6.94	6.57	6.77	8.00	7.11	7.12	6.32	7.18	6.76	7.21	7.06	6.68
		n	225	225	223	226	213	197	183	213	176	176	176	173	183	183	183	183	
	Female	Mean	7.75	6.70	7.07	6.51	7.62	7.11	7.01	6.88	8.37	7.28	7.10	6.50	7.94	7.43	7.39	7.47	7.39
		n	315	318	311	316	307	279	267	310	303	305	305	302	275	275	275	275	
≥50 years	Male	Mean	7.81	7.15	7.17	5.88	8.02	7.09	6.43	6.54	8.28	7.62	7.33	5.87	7.27	7.31	7.04	6.74	6.98
		n	107	108	104	102	114	110	92	113	119	119	118	115	140	140	140	140	
	Female	Mean	7.97	7.45	7.52	6.11	8.19	7.29	7.38	6.67	8.67	8.03	7.65	6.31	7.96	7.68	7.37	7.25	7.28
		n	132	137	129	128	161	142	141	159	211	214	208	203	204	204	204	204	

L, Love; I, Insight; F, Fortitude; E, Engagement; HI, Happiness Index.
1 Notice that females enjoy higher LIFE scores in almost every year from 2008, for both the younger group and for the 50 and above group.
2 Notice that for both males and females the older groups generally have higher scores in LIF, but a lower score in E.
*Average for the years.

Table 5.2 Regression results using 2008–2012 telephone survey pooled data (with yearly dummies) from Hong Kong

Dependent variable: happiness	Coefficient	t-statistic
Love	0.18	6.71
Insight	0.20	6.83
Fortitude	0.14	6.35
Engagement	0.25	9.91
Age 30–49 years	−0.23	−2.68
Age 50 up	−0.26	−2.62
Female	0.11	2.01
Married	0.16	2.09
Divorced	−0.47	−1.84
Widowed	0.45	1.39
Financial stress	−0.30	−7.41
Household income lower than HK$10K	−0.10	−0.88
Household income HK$40K or more	0.08	1.22
Monthly income not reported	−0.04	−0.65
2009	0.09	1.06
2010	−0.20	−1.82
2011	−0.24	−2.35
2012	−0.23	−2.71
Constant term	2.28	11.31
Number of observations = 2,999		
$F(18, 2980) = 61.75$		
Probability $> F = 0$		
R-squared = 0.3642		

Dummy for 2008 has been left out and serves as the benchmark for year effects.

income variable (for HK$40,000[8]) even carries a negative, though insignificant coefficient.

Similar results are obtained from an online survey that was conducted in 2011 (Table 5.3). We had over 8,500 valid responses, but dropping those that contain missing variables, we had 5,272 observations for the regression exercise.[9]

Testing the LIFE formula using the World Value Survey

In order to test the validity of the 'happiness formula' as Love + Insight + Fortitude + Engagement, we use the data from the World Value Survey that cover many countries across different cultures. We compiled indices of Love, Insight, Fortitude and Engagement based on some subsets of the questions asked. It should be noted that the questions are not custom-designed for my research, and are chosen on the basis of their bearing some resemblance to the central concepts of Love, Insight, Fortitude and Engagement.

Table 5.3 Regression results using online survey (2011) data from Hong Kong

Dependent variable: happiness	Coefficient	t-score
Love	0.18	10.25
Insight	0.25	10.75
Fortitude	0.17	6.64
Engagement	0.32	13.62
Age 30–49	−0.14	−3.09
Age 50 up	−0.18	−2.42
Female	0.25	6.73
Married	0.22	4.85
Divorced	−0.40	−3.06
Widowed	−0.36	−1.69
Education	−0.06	−4.78
Unemployed	−0.38	−3.27
Financial stress	−0.47	−15.08
Household income < HK$10K	−0.05	−0.89
Household income ≥ HK$40K	−0.06	−1.49
Constant term	1.16	7.13
Number of observations = 5,272		
$F(15,5256) = 301.18$		
Probability > F = 0.0000		
R-squared = 0.5197		

Notes
Education: a scale variable from no formal education to university.
Income earners from HK$10,000 to just below HK$40,000 per month are left out to serve as a benchmark.

The questions in the World Value Survey on which the LIFE scores are constructed, as well as the way the scores are compiled, are laid out in Appendix table 5.7.

Table 5.4 shows the results on the baseline model, with happiness regressed on only the LIFE variables. The estimation is based on a sample of 52,693 observations, each of which represents one person who responded to all the relevant questions. The regression shows how the happiness index is related to the LIFE scores statistically.

The figures in the coefficient column show the estimated effect of each of the LIFE variables on the happiness score. It shows that Love carries the biggest coefficient, followed by Engagement. Given that all scores have been converted to the 0–10 scale, someone with one point more in the Love score will on average enjoy 0.18 points higher on the happiness scale. All coefficients on LIFE score variables are statistically significant at 1 per cent.

Table 5.5 shows the results of a bigger model, with demographic and economic variables included along with the LIFE variables. Again all LIFE variables carry statistically significant coefficients. The sample is reduced to 42,514 observations.

Table 5.4 Baseline regression on World Value Survey wave 4 data (2005)

Dependent variable: happiness	Coefficient	t-score
Love	0.18	19.34
Insight	0.08	8.77
Fortitude	0.10	20.12
Engagement	0.13	22.1
Constant term	3.68	40.45

Number of observations = 52,693
$F(4, 52688) = 441.68$
Probability $> F = 0.0000$
R-squared = 0.034

Females are found to be happier, as are the married and the relatively high-income people. Age has a U-shaped effect on happiness, first declining and then rising.

Table 5.5 World Value Survey results (wave 4) with effects of demographic variables and other variables added

Dependent variable: happiness		
	Observations = 42,514	
	$F(19, 42494) = 204.28$	
	Probabiltiy $> F = 0.0000$	
	Adjusted R-squared = 0.0893	
	Coefficient	t-statistic
Love	0.16	15.47
Insight	0.10	9.99
Fortitude	0.07	13.83
Engagement	0.12	17.61
Female	0.12	5.38
Age	−0.06	−12.07
Age squared	0.00	11.27
Education	0.08	3.68
Education squared	−0.01	−3.64
Married	0.22	5.98
Cohabitation	0.3	6.38
Divorced	−0.3	−4.14
Separated	−0.26	−2.82
Widowed	−0.54	−8.32
With child/children	0.06	7.76
Self-employed	0.05	1.54
Retired	−0.28	−5.92
Unemployed	−0.49	−11.18
Relative income	0.18	33.33
Constant term	3.89	26.62

52 The happiness formula

Finally, we add country dummies, and the results are presented in Table 5.6, where the country coefficients are not reported. Standard errors are recalculated to be clustered at country level and thus allow for intercountry variations:

We may observe that the LIFE variables continue to be highly significant. Happiness is seen to be positively associated with marriage and (self-reported perceived) relative income. Age appears to have first a negative effect on happiness and then a positive effect, confirming the well-known result of a U-shaped profile of happiness

Table 5.6 World Value Survey results (wave 4) with country variables included and year dummies added (2005–2008): ordinary least squares result (errors clustered at country level)

Dependent variable: happiness	Observations = 42,514 $F(18,42495) = 405.48$ Probability > F = 0.0000 Adjusted R-squared = 0.1715	
	Coefficient	t-statistic
Love	0.13	7.81
Insight	0.06	3.59
Fortitude	0.05	4.82
Engagement	0.09	6.52
Female	0.09	2.21
Age (excluding those below 18)	−0.06	−7.2
Age squared	0.00	6.34
Education	0.09	2.01
Education squared	−0.01	−1.86
Married	0.45	6.96
Cohabitation	0.22	3.98
Divorced	−0.16	−2.22
Separated	−0.32	−3.11
Widowed	−0.19	−2.5
With child/children	0.02	1.87
Self-employed	−0.07	−1.59
Retired	−0.09	−1.29
Unemployed	−0.39	−4.26
Relative income	0.17	7.95
Year 2005	−0.31	−9.64
Year 2006	−0.74	−20.2
Year 2007	−0.63	−7
Constant term	5.28	15.14

Notes
The year 2008 has been dropped and serves as a benchmark for the year dummies. Country variables are subject to data availability and include: Andorra, Australia, Brazil, Bulgaria, Burkina Faso, Chile, China, Cyprus, Egypt, Ethiopia, Finland, Georgia, Germany-East, Germany-West, Ghana, India, Indonesia, Malaysia, Mali, Mexico, Moldova, Norway, Peru, Poland, Serbia, Slovenia, Spain, Romania, Rwanda, South Africa, South Korea, Sweden, Taiwan, Thailand, Trinidad, Turkey, Ukraine, Uruguay, Vietnam, Zambia).

over the life cycle. This result appears to be at odds with the earlier results reported based on Hong Kong data, but the specification of the equation is slightly different as age squared is now adopted instead of age bracket dummies. The effects of ageing on health may just not yet show up under this specification. Interestingly, education brings benefits in terms of benefits initially but higher education appears to result in lower happiness. Unemployment has a significant negative effect on happiness. Adjusted R-squared goes up to 17.15 per cent.

Conclusions

It takes time and effort to build up mental capital. The scores on Love, Insight, Fortitude and Engagement reflect people's mental capital and have been found to be associated with a happy, fulfilling life. The qualities underlying these scores are related to personality and are in part inborn. But they are certainly not immutable. Most people learn to love more as they age, and tend to find new meanings in life (Mogilner et al., 2011), acquire a new understanding of what success in life is all about and become wiser. The Hong Kong surveys suggest that among Love, Insight, Fortitude and Engagement, Engagement is the only element among the four elements in LIFE that does not seem to grow with age. The same surveys suggest that women appear to have higher LIFE scores than men, especially among those before 50. Women in particular appear to be naturally more loving than men, but with age men gradually learn to love more, and also become wiser.[10] Figure 5.1

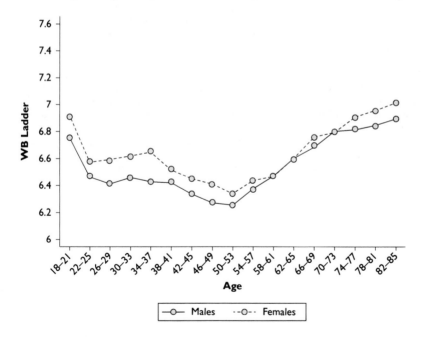

Figure 5.1 Wellbeing (WB) – age profile in the United States.
Source: Stone et al. (2010).

shows that in the United States men's happiness is lower than women's before the age of 60 but rises faster than women's in their 50s, finally overtaking them by 60–65. This rise is likely to be related to the tendency of their scores of Love, Insight and Fortitude to rise with age at a somewhat faster rate.

Notes

1 For example, the key Eurofound happiness question is: 'How happy would you say you are these days?' www.eurofound.europa.eu/surveys/smt/eqls/2eqls_03_13.htm.
2 Temperament is usually taken to be those characteristics in a person's disposition of a person that one is born with, while personality is more inclusive, comprising 'the entire mental organization of a human being at any stage of his development'. 'It embraces every phase of human character: intellect, temperament, skill, morality, and every attitude that has been built up in the course of one's life' (Warren and Carmichael, 1930, p. 333). We are using the terms more loosely to refer to what Warren and Carmichael called 'personality'.
3 See David T. Lykken (no date), 'The Heritability of Happiness,' *Harvard Mental Health Letter*, downloadable from: www.psych.umn.edu/psylabs/happness/hapindex.htm.
4 See BBC news report: news.bbc.co.uk/2/hi/programmes/happiness_formula/4783836.stm.
5 See Lykken in www.psych.umn.edu/psylabs/happness/hapindex.htm.
6 I follow the translation by Lok Sang Ho in *Human Spirituality and Happiness* (2011a).
7 Frijters and Beatton (2012) challenged the U-shaped happiness profile as a result of researchers not having controlled for fixed effects and for age-related selectivity and reporting problems. Once the effects were properly controlled, they found 'quite a sharp decline around the age of 75'.
8 This translates to roughly US$61,000 in yearly income.
9 OLS results are presented rather than ordered probit results. Usually for regressions with the dependent variable confined to a scale, ordered probit is more appropriate to avoid predicted values going beyond the permissible range. In practice, however, this problem seldom arises for our regressions, and OLS makes for easier interpretation.
10 The evidence from the 2011 Lingnan University Online Survey, which covers over 8,500 respondents, shows that Love and Insight scores among men rise quite quickly and faster than women's after 50. The telephone surveys, which cover a much smaller sample, do not show the same pattern though.

Appendix Table 5.7 LIFE score definitions based on World Value Survey wave 4 data

Question	Love	Insight	Fortitude	Engagement
1.	Putting more emphasis on family is:	I seek to be myself rather than to follow others	Hard work in the long run brings success	Important in life: to be creative and to do things one's own way
Scale	A bad/a neutral/a good thing (scale 1–3)	Strongly disagree … strongly agree (scale 1–4)	Not true at all … usually true (scale 1–10)	Not like me … very much like me (scale 1–6)
2.	Progress toward a less impersonal and more humane society is of:	I make a lot of effort to live up to what my friends expect	Belief in one's ability to change destiny	How important in life: politics
Scale	Lowest rank … highest rank among several choices (scale 1–3)	Strongly agree … strongly disagree (scale 1–4)	Total belief in fate … total belief in ability to shape destiny (scale 1–10)	Not important … very important (scale 1–4)
3.		I decide my goals in life by myself		Importance in life: work
Scale		Strongly disagree … strongly agree (scale 1–4)		Not important … very important (scale 1–4)
4.		Importance in life: to be rich		
Scale		Not like me … very much like me (scale 1–6)		
5.		Importance in life: to look after environment		
Scale		Not like me … very much like me (scale 1–6)		

LIFE, Love, Insight, Fortitude, Engagement.
All scores as well as their components are rescaled to the 11-point 0–10 scale and are averaged to obtain the LIFE scores using the equation specified below.
New variable = (original variable − 1) * [(new scale number of points − 1)/(original scale number of points − 1)]
The original variable is assumed to take on values starting from 1. If it starts from zero, there would be no need to subtract 1 before multiplying with the conversion factor.

Chapter 6

Marriage, mental capital and happiness

Introduction

Many studies have indicated a positive 'marriage premium' on happiness. That is, married people appear to be happier. Tables 5.5 and 5.6, based on the World Value Survey, also confirm this. The causality between happiness and marriage, however, is not very clear. In principle, happier people tend to relate to people better, and stand a better chance of finding a marriage partner. So happier people are more likely to get married than unhappy people. This is similar to the argument that, while success makes people happy, happiness may also breed success.

Analysis of data from Hong Kong indicates that for males the marriage premium tends to fade with age. That is, older married males do not appear to be happier than single males of the same age. This suggests that for men marriage may not matter that much to happiness over the long run. For females, the results appear mixed. In one survey the marriage premium in happiness is higher for older women than for younger women. In another the marriage premium is smaller for older women.

All this, however, hides much of the truth, which is that marriage can indeed bring some people more happiness, while marriage may not bring happiness to others, and may even bring unhappiness to yet others.

A crucial question therefore is how to enhance the chances of a 'successful' marriage, in the sense that it enhances the happiness of the married couple. At the very least, marriage should not make people less happy. What is the key?

Mental capital is the key to happy marriages

Table 6.1 shows a comparison of LIFE scores and happiness indices from an online survey conducted in 2011 between single and married people. It is quite clear that married people consistently have higher LIFE scores and happiness scores than single people, for both the below-45 and the 45 and above groups.

Both men and women gain more Love, Insight, Fortitude and Engagement as they grow older, regardless of whether they are single or married. This pattern is exactly the same as that indicated in the telephone surveys. The biggest difference between the telephone surveys and the online survey is that, while the telephone

Table 6.1 LIFE scores between single and married by age (online survey 2011)

Both sexes	Below 45		45 or above	
	Single	Married	Single	Married
	(4,710)	(2,370)	(184)	(953)
Love	7.27	7.80	7.62	8.07
Insight	6.57	7.08	7.20	7.42
Fortitude	7.37	7.66	7.59	7.84
Engagement	7.03	7.45	7.23	7.67
Happiness Index	6.79	7.56	7.23	7.67

LIFE, Love, Insight, Fortitude, Engagement.

surveys show that *females consistently outperform males* in LIFE, the online survey shows stronger male performance in Insight, Fortitude and Engagement. This is probably related to the self-selection bias in the online sample.

Table 6.2 shows LIFE and happiness scores among single and married people, by sex and by age. It shows that, among married people, males' LIFE scores advance faster than those of females with age. Following the hypothesis that the marriage premium is likely to be higher the higher the marriage partner's LIFE scores, the pattern of greater marriage premiums for older females than for younger females, and that of greater marriage premiums for older females than for older men is not surprising (Table 6.3).

In the event of a divorce, younger males appear to suffer more than females, while older females appear to suffer more than older males (relative to married people).

Table 6.2 LIFE scores in Hong Kong by sex, age and marital status 2011, online data

Male	Below 45		45 or above	
	Single	Married	Single	Married
	(1,614)	(802)	(59)	(459)
Love	7.14	7.62	7.77	8.07
Insight	6.75	7.09	7.53	7.51
Fortitude	7.49	7.60	7.68	7.82
Engagement	7.18	7.41	7.60	7.72
Happiness Index	6.71	7.19	7.59	7.61

Female	Below 45		45 or above	
	Single	Married	Single	Married
	(3,096)	(1,568)	(125)	(494)
Love	7.34	7.89	7.55	8.06
Insight	6.47	7.08	7.05	7.33
Fortitude	7.31	7.69	7.55	7.86
Engagement	6.95	7.47	7.06	7.63
Happiness Index	6.83	7.75	7.06	7.72

LIFE, Love, Insight, Fortitude, Engagement.

Note: Brackets indicate number of observations. Shaded boxes indicate higher scores than those of the other sex.

Table 6.3 Gender and marriage status effects on happiness/discounts (online survey)

	Male < 45 (i)	Female < 45 (ii)	Female premium (iii) = (ii) − (i)	Male ≥ 45 (iv)	Female ≥ 45 (v)	Female premium (vi) = (v) − (iv)
Total of relevant coefficients for single (a)	0	0.283	0.283	0.268	0.133	−0.135
Total of relevant coefficients for married (b)	0.226	0.504	0.278	0.248	0.390	0.142
Total of relevant coefficients for divorced (c)	−0.689	−0.145	0.544	0.0655	−0.073	−0.138
Premium of married over single (d) = (b) − (a)	0.226	0.220	−0.005	−0.020	0.257	0.277
Premium of married over divorced† (e) = (b) − (c)	0.915	0.649	−0.266	0.183	0.463	0.280
Premium of divorced over single (f) = (c) − (a)	−0.689	0.365	1.054	−0.233	−0.206	0.027

Notes
The total coefficients are derived by summing up relevant coefficients in non-interactive and interactive dummies. This table is derived from Appendix Table 6.5.
† The larger the number, the stronger the adverse effect of divorce. A negative number would imply positive effect.

Where there is a divorce, it is likely that it is because of a deficiency in mental capital, and under the circumstances breaking up may be wise for the one with stronger mental capital, but it probably hurts more for the spouse with weaker mental capital.

Following the hypothesis that marriage premiums tend to be higher when the marriage partner has higher LIFE scores, given that the telephone surveys all showed that females have higher LIFE scores, males should have higher marriage premiums than females. This is borne out by Table 6.4, which is calculated from a similar regression, as presented in Appendix Table 6.5, using pooled telephone survey results.

Romantic affinity and love

It is useful to distinguish between '*romantic affinity*' and *love*. Although Zick Rubin (1970) used the term *romantic love* conceptually romantic affinity is *not* love. When a young man meets a young woman for the first time and suddenly 'falls in love with her', he really has only a strong romantic affinity for the woman. Since it is the first meeting, how can there be a love for the woman that is so different from love for other people? Does he really care for the wellbeing of the woman? I have heard of stories of young men and women 'loving each other' so much that they committed suicide together when something got in the way of them being together. Can this be love?

Rubin did explicitly specify caring for each other as one of the elements of 'romantic love.' But love and romantic affinity are altogether two different things.

Table 6.4 Gender and marriage status effects on happiness/discounts (telephone surveys)

	Male age < 45 (i)	Female age < 45 (ii)	Female premium (iii) = (ii) − (i)	Male age ≥ 45 (iv)	Female age ≥ 45 (v)	Female premium (vi) = (v) − (iv)
Total of relevant coefficients for single (a)	0	0.559	0.559	0.341	0.533	0.192
Total of relevant coefficients for married (b)	0.279	0.585	0.306	0.364	0.300	−0.064
Total of relevant coefficients for divorced (c)	−0.112	−1.878	−1.99	1.259	−1.026	−2.285
Premium of married over single (d) = (b) − (a)	0.279	0.026	−0.253	0.023	−0.233	−0.256
Premium of married over divorced[†] (e) = (b) − (c)	0.391	1.904	1.513	−0.895	1.326	2.221
Premium of divorced over single (f) = (c) − (a)	−0.112	−2.437	−2.325	0.918	−1.559	−2.477

Notes
The total coefficients to capture the total effects are derived by summing up relevant coefficients in non-interactive and interactive dummies. For example, married male over 45 = sum of 0.3411, −0.2562, and 0.2789.
[†] The larger the number, the stronger the adverse effect of divorce. A negative number would imply positive effect.

Two lovers can of course genuinely love and care for each other, and they can also share a strong affinity for each other. They may express their love for each other in ways different from how parents express their love for their children, particularly but not exclusively through an intimate sexual relationship. But even though the ways of *expressing love* may vary depending on the relationship, the nature of the love is really the same. It remains a genuine care for the feeling and wellbeing of the beloved person.

The romantic affinity between a couple can of course develop into true love. When true love takes hold, however, it must have transcended the relationship. This means that if you really love a woman, you would like her to make decisions that are good for her over the long term. Suppose she decides to leave you for another man, and you know that that man truly loves her and is likely to bring her happiness: if you truly loved her you would give her your blessing. Suppose she fell seriously ill: you would take good care of her just as a mother would take good care of her child if the child became seriously ill.

Division of labour within the household

Recent data in the United States indicate that the traditional female premium over male in happiness has narrowed so much that it has virtually disappeared (Stevenson and Wolfers, 2009). These authors, citing Kahneman (1999), suggested that it might have to do with more honest reporting, as women enjoying better economic wellbeing and social status became more ready to deflate their previously inflated responses. Moreover, 'increased opportunities available to women may have increased what women require to declare themselves happy'. 'Finally, the changes brought about through the women's movement may have decreased women's happiness. The increased opportunity to succeed in many dimensions may have led to an increased likelihood of believing that one's life is not measuring up'(p. 223). None of these explanations is really convincing. It appears to me that the rise in women's participation in the labour force plus the generally greater responsibilities of married women in taking up household chores than men is a key reason behind the decline in women's happiness relative to men. As was pointed out by a University of Michigan study in 2005, before they had children married women did 17 hours of housework a week as compared with 7 hours for men. After they had children, married women with more than three kids recorded an average of about 28 hours of housework a week, while married men with more than three kids logged only about 10 hours of housework a week, a difference of 18 hours per week. 'This study shows with men and women working, men still lag women in housework.'[1]

While excessive housework hours for women could be a key reason why women's premium over men's on happiness has fallen markedly, the solution is not necessarily 'Let's divide up the work equally and rotate.' As Paula Szuchman and Jenny Anderson (2011) advised in *Spousonomics: Using Economics to Master Love, Marriage, and Dirty Dishes*, husbands and wives should divide up the work along principles of comparative advantage, and should not focus so much on equality as such. This is not to suggest that equality is unimportant. Equality is very important, but only in the sense of giving full respect for the other person as a person, as we do ourselves, and not in the sense of being very calculating to make sure that equality in some measure is achieved. Equality is an attitude. That indeed is one of the essentials of Love and Insight. What is needed to make a happy marriage is to build up mental capital in the form of Love, Insight, Fortitude and Engagement.

Thus it is not just the hours of housework on top of a fulltime job that affect women's happiness. More often there is the expectation that women are supposed to take up more of the household chores that gives rise to a feeling of unfairness or alienation. Putting down such expectations, and letting the one with the comparative advantage do each household chore is really the best strategy and a sign of wisdom and mastery of the economics of love. Better still, treat the household 'chore' not as a 'chore', but as something that each happily takes up for the benefit of the family. This would nurture the 'mental good' of love or loving kindness.

Conclusions

Married people statistically are more likely to be happier than unmarried people, but marriage does not always bring greater happiness. A successful marriage depends on the mental capital of the couple. Being married to someone who has more mental capital than oneself is likely to bring increased happiness. Being married to someone who has very little mental capital, or has negative mental capital, could be the beginning of a nightmare. What matters most to the success of a marriage is mental capital. Children of parents with strong mental capital will likely develop strong mental capital.[2] Similarly, children of parents with weak mental capital will likely inherit the weak mental capital. Understanding the importance and the nature of mental capital will save many marriages, and perhaps avoid many unsuccessful marriages, and will help foster a generation of happier, healthier individuals.

Notes

1 www.nsf.gov/discoveries/disc_summ.jsp?cntn_id=111458.
2 See Ho (2013), where evidence was found that children of parents who enjoy good spousal relations appear to be more loving.

Appendix Table 6.5 Online survey 2011 full model results

Ordinary least squares	Observations = 7111 $F(18,7092) = 327.13$ Probability > F = 0.0000 R-squared = 0.5135	
	Coefficient	t-statistic
Love	0.16133	10.84
Insight	0.24630	12.43
Fortitude	0.16178	7.75
Engagement	0.33885	17.05
Household income over 40K*	−0.10952	−3.24
Household income below 10K*	−0.06201	−1.11
Financial stress	−0.44449	−16.95
Female	0.28342	5.84
Female and married	0.22016	5.26
Female and over 45	−0.15041	−1.34
Female and over 45 and married	0.37132	0.3
Male and married	0.22553	3.81
Male and over 45	0.26824	2.25
Male and over 45 and married	−0.24559	−1.8
Female and divorced	−0.42862	−2.72
Male and divorced	−0.68916	−2.07
Female and over 45 and divorced	0.22278	0.97
Male and over 45 and divorced	0.48645	1.17
Constant term	0.71691	5.94

*Monthly household incomes in HK$; HK$7.8 roughly translates to US$1.

Chapter 7

More on mental goods
Self-actualisation versus vanity

Introduction

Abraham Maslow in his discussion on the hierarchy of needs put self-actualisation as one of the higher aspirations of humankind. Self-actualisation is realising the potential within, or bringing that potential into reality. For anyone who has experienced it, self-actualisation is a wonderful experience in and of itself, but incidental to self-actualisation is the mental good called 'sense of achievement'. When people take self-actualisation to be an end in itself, the aspiration is 'higher' on the needs hierarchy, in the sense that, while it is not seen to be as basic as survival, the degree of satisfaction achieved can be very great. Still, while some people seek self-actualisation as a natural yearning, others may seek achievement in order to win acceptance or recognition by others. For them the sense of achievement or dignity is built on recognition by others. Some people would call this 'vanity', but the presumed value judgement is not warranted. 'Vanity' carries the connotation that such pursuit is morally wrong. But there is nothing wrong with desiring mental goods, since such desires are universal. What is more pertinent is that self-actualisation is generally more reliable and more effective as a source of happiness than vanity.

Self-actualisation is more reliable than vanity because it does not depend on the behaviour or the performance of others. One can 'self-actualise' without worrying about falling behind others, but the 'achievement' based on vanity is lost when others overtake us, or when others simply do not want to take notice.

Because performing better than others and getting others' recognition based on outstanding performance is so hard, many people take the easy way out by conspicuous consumption and by displaying their wealth and status. Still others may derive satisfaction from being recognised as a benefactor for others.

On the other hand the self-actualisers gain happiness without regard to what others think and do. Because they do not have to be outstanding in order to self-actualise, self-actualisation is actually the easier way to achieve happiness!

Loving or vain parents

Most parents derive a lot of satisfaction from seeing their children make notable achievements. This may reflect two kinds of emotions, which can coexist. First is a genuine relief and joy that their beloved children could do so well. Second is the thought that the children's achievements reflect their own achievements as parents. Vain parents are those who push their children in directions consistent with what they think constitutes success – which is generally what their peers consider to be success – against the best interest of their children.

Whether vanity is involved, however, all parents require a sense of achievement. Loving parents differ from vain parents in that they see achievement differently. Loving parents derive a sense of achievement when they see their children live a fulfilling life. Vain parents derive a sense of achievement when they see their children accomplish what their peers consider to be remarkable achievements. So they have different 'production functions' for the mental good called sense of achievement. As discussed before, these differences in production functions reflect differences in culture.

As far as the parents themselves are concerned, the difference in production functions need not matter that much to parents' sense of achievement. However, they produce different effects on the children. In one case, with loving parents, children pursue their own goals, and thus enjoy a sense of autonomy. They also are likely to sense the love of their parents. With vain parents, children pursue the goals identified by their parents, and they suffer a loss of autonomy. They may sense that their parents are selfish, and are likely to live an unhappy life. Using the jargon of economists, as vain parents produce and acquire their sense of achievement, they produce an external cost on their children. This is a 'technological externality', because a 'mental bad' in the form of loss of autonomy is produced, adversely affecting the welfare of the children.

Sense of achievement and the nature of achievement

What constitutes achievement varies from person to person and is conditioned by the social environment and culture. For many people, and in many societies, achievement means distinction or outperforming others. This thinking is common in highly competitive societies. While it is commonly believed that competition helps push standards higher and forges progress, it may also give rise to serious social, economic and psychological problems. There is a distinction between healthy competition and ruthless competition.

Two of the most striking ills from excessive emphasis on competition are doping and excessive, even inhumane training for the Olympic Games. While the spirit of the Olympic Games has always been held to be friendly and fair competition, doping has had a long history. Winning a medal, particularly a gold medal, is a big deal. Many countries give gold medallists huge financial rewards. Since first place and second place translate into vastly different rewards, it is not surprising that some athletes resort to unfair competition. With all the eyes of one's compatriots focused on whether one wins the gold medal, winning the gold medal is taken to be a big achievement. But honestly, if the gold medal is won through cheating, is that an achievement? How much satisfaction does the achievement offer?

In contrast to winning the gold medal, some people quietly achieve with hard work without making a fuss. There are some lone rock climbers who tackle very difficult cliffs and their success is known only to themselves. In 1984, a Frenchman, Patrick Bauer, decided to embark on a self-sufficient 350-km journey across the Algerian desert on foot. It took him over 12 days. Having completed the journey, he figured that other people could share his passion. So in 1986 he began to organise an ultramarathon, which then attracted 23 participants. Since then it has become an annual event, and in the course of 28 years it has attracted more than 12,000 participants. Today the Marathon des Sables is a major endurance event that has been copied by several other races. Each year, moreover, the event is oversubscribed and one may have to wait a year or two to be admitted to a race.

Billed as 'the toughest race on earth', a CNN report began asking:

> Would you pay thousands of dollars to spend seven days running under the scorching sun of the Sahara Desert, traversing shifting sand dunes and punishing rocky plateaus for more than 220 kilometers, with all your food and kit affixed to your back?

The economist would logically conclude that:

> the utility of meeting the challenge, and that of the prospect of meeting the challenge, must be greater than the sum of the disutility of the stressful training and the tough run itself and the financial cost needed to participate in the race.

'Achievement' to Patrick Bauer and to those who participate in the race must involve a kind of satisfaction 'that money can't buy'. These people would certainly not cheat to 'achieve'. Cheating cannot be achievement. These people find satisfaction in overcoming difficulties, and this most probably has little to do with getting others' recognition.

Conclusions

My colleague Professor Simon Fan argues that vanity is humanity's greatest motivation. I do not dispute that vanity indeed explains much of human behaviour, but I also believe that human beings often simply do things that are natural to them. Some children take up music, painting, dancing, collecting, and other hobbies quite naturally. As they grow up, they indeed will be acculturated to the ways of life of their peers, to different degrees. While others will bend themselves to meet others' expectations, some will continue to be themselves. In the end, it is those who follow their own calling who tend to be happier. Being oneself is a big achievement in life, and requires both courage and stamina.

Chapter 8

Insight

Insight: Wisdom is...

Wisdom is to know the grand purpose.
The grand purpose is to realize Life's potential.
That requires taming our ancient weaknesses.
To be wise is to overcome mind's sicknesses.

Wisdom is a sense of proportion.
A sense of proportion is to abandon excesses:
Giving up the urge to keep seeking more;
To be wise is to be free from this scourge.

Wisdom is being able to tell means from ends.
That requires knowing what you really want.
You certainly want to achieve your goal.
But a goal does not mean much unless it serves your soul.

Wisdom is to see the transient nature of things,
To realize everything is but the result of transient causes and conditions;
The self as we know it should only be an instrument
To serve the master, like a servant.

Wisdom is never to worry,
When worrying doesn't do you any good.
Most worrying is really nonsense.
Why not simply do your best, and live in good conscience?

Wisdom is to live fully.
To live fully is to find value in every moment of your life
Even when it brings sorrow and pain.
A day truly lived is a day truly gained.

(Ho, 2011a)

Introduction

Economists understand that reaching the maximum value of an 'objective function' – whether it is a profit function or a utility function – means climbing up the hill as long as the next step is up and stopping when the next step is down. 'Never overdo' is a dictum to be followed; just as 'Never fall short' is one.

But wisdom is certainly much more than merely finding the maximum value of something which is at most a means to a final goal. Insight requires a good sense of proportion, seeing the big picture, and the ability to distinguish between ends and means. We want to make the most out of our lives. This must be the most important objective. In comparison, making money, as well as building a career, must be considered only instrumental: we make money or build a career only as long as doing so helps enrich our lives.

Wisdom must be about taking command, rather than allowing our fate to be dictated by circumstances or by instincts. Given the nature of instincts, breaking away from them when they fail to serve us is not easy at all. Disciplining the mind, and overcoming our own weaknesses and thus taking command of ourselves, must be central to wisdom. Because of inertia, however, the mind keeps wandering around and is extremely difficult to control. This is the rationale for 'mindfulness training', which Seligman also mentioned in his book, *Authentic Happiness*.

Wisdom is also about knowing what you can control and what you cannot, then focusing on doing the best within what you can control, and not worrying about the factors that are totally beyond your control. We have already discussed the subject of real versus false constraints in the last chapter, but need to reiterate the importance of not worrying about what we cannot control. Such worries would only undermine our happiness and our ability to realise the best that is within our control.

Wisdom is about being truthful and honest about our feelings. Reflecting truly on our experience and trying to do better next time while remaining truthful about ourselves is living truthfully. 'A day truly lived is a day truly gained.'

But there is one facet of Insight that needs further elaboration. This is the subject of obsession, which is a common and basic human weakness. We will first discuss the nature of obsession, and then go on to the subject of how to free ourselves from obsession.

Obsessions and 'the seven deadly sins'

Obsession refers to the enslavement of the mind as it is dominated by a persistent object of desire or fear, which can be physical or mental. Obsessions may vary in intensity, and the object of obsessions may also vary, from the mundane to the lofty. But desire-related obsessions share the commonality of stubbornly focusing and insisting on the pursuance of something, some experience, or some episode, and in doing so making a huge sacrifice in terms of the person's overall long-term welfare. Obsessions result in obsessive-compulsive disorders.

One mild form of obsession is the idea, which often lingers in our subconscious mind, that since certain things belong to us, losing them is unacceptable. A sense of loss is a 'mental bad'. This explains the so-called endowment effect in behavioural economics, which refers to the often-found result that people tend to require more compensation to part with something they already have than the price they are willing to pay to acquire that something.[1] Because the endowment effect is so commonly observed, we may say that human beings tend to be obsessed with objects owned to the extent that giving them up engenders a mental bad.

We can begin with the so-called 'seven deadly sins': wrath, greed, sloth, pride, lust, envy and gluttony.

Wrath is a more violent form of anger. It is generally a result of frustration, and frustration occurs when what is intended fails to materialise. The excessive focus is on the goal. The frustration of not achieving an identified goal produces wrath. When anger takes over, a person might do destructive things, and could hurt himself and others.

Greed is a strong desire to obtain more material goods. The excessive focus is on the material objects of the cravings. When greed takes over, again the person could ignore other people's welfare altogether, while the burning desire for more makes him restless and unhappy. Behaviour motivated by greed could lead to a loss of welfare for others as well as for himself.

Sloth is failing to garner what lies within a person's ability to improve his own wellbeing or that of others. The person is a slave to his own inertia, and too focused on the difficulties that may beset him.

Pride is an excessive sense of the ego, which blinds a person to his own inadequacies. The opposite of pride is humility. With humility, one can gradually develop one's latent strengths. With pride, weaknesses are preserved while the latent abilities continue to be undeveloped.

Lust is an excessive pursuit of the pleasures of sex, which blinds a person from seeing and developing other possibilities.

Envy[2] is a sense of relative deprivation, caused by an excessive focus on oneself, so that seeing others achieving something desirable causes a loss in happiness.

Gluttony is simply excessive indulgence in material goods and services, which again blinds one from the many other good things that life can offer.

These are 'deadly sins' not because they are so defined by moralists, but because they ultimately prevent us from achieving a richer, more fulfilling life, as defined by ourselves and not by moralists. Evidence abounds that people under the grip of these 'deadly sins' are unhappy. They are unhappy because they find themselves totally out of their own control. They are no longer masters of themselves.

Pseudo mental goods

It may appear strange to us that some people appear to enjoy the very opposite of the mental goods that most people cherish. If human nature is universal, how do we explain some people's taking pleasure at seeing others suffer and be humiliated? Admittedly, there is still controversy among psychologists about the origin of such behaviour. A possible explanation is that when individuals fail to get or are denied a mental good they may develop an instinct of pursuing the very opposite of what they have been denied, so that sadism is actually loving kindness transmuted into its very opposite. Loving kindness is a mental good that every person would aspire to by nature. When denied or deprived of it, the individual desperately needs something in its place, and that something is the very opposite of loving kindness. A person denied autonomy or unable to realise autonomy may turn his natural desire for autonomy into a desire to control others. These transmutations of the original mental goods can be called *'pseudo mental goods'*, and are potentially very dangerous because once the 'pseudo mental capital' takes hold it is very difficult to eradicate it, and it can then become very destructive. Erich Fromm called an extreme form of this behaviour *malignant narcissism* and referred to it as a severe mental sickness representing 'the quintessence of evil'. He characterised the condition as 'the most severe pathology and the root of the most vicious destructiveness and inhumanity',[3] leading to a descent into *necrophilia*, literally a love of death as a result of a failure to come to terms with life.

I call these transmutations of mental goods *'pseudo mental goods'* because, although people do derive a momentary pleasure or satisfaction from them, their minds are not really at peace. With an impulsive urge to hurt and manipulate others, they end up making a mess of their own lives and those of many others.

Obsessions: excessive attachment in romance

Zick Rubin (1970) thinks that romantic love must involve a strong and even obsessive sense of attachment. Here are a few passages from *Romeo and Juliet* to illustrate the strong affinity.

> One fairer than my love? The all-seeing sun
> Ne'er saw her match since first the world begun.
> (Act I Scene II)

> T'is torture, and not mercy. Heaven is here
> Where Juliet lives, and every cat and dog
> And little mouse, every unworthy thing,
> Live here in heaven and may look on her,
> But Romeo may not.
> (Act III Scene III)

In desperation, when Romeo mistook Juliet's fake death for real, Romeo sought to kill himself, saying:

> Well, Juliet, I will lie with thee to-night.
> Let's see for means: O mischief, thou art swift
> To enter in the thoughts of desperate men!
> (Act V Scene I)

Then, upon discovering that Romeo was dead, Juliet could not find the courage to live by herself. Before stabbing herself, and hearing that someone was coming, she said:

> Yea, noise? then I'll be brief. O happy dagger!
> (snatching Romeo's dagger)
> This is thy sheath;
> (stabs herself)
> there rust, and let me die.
> (falls on Romeo's body, and dies)
> (Act V Scene III)

Stories like *Romeo and Juliet* in the west and the *Butterfly Lovers* in the east really share the same theme: in each case the young man would rather die than live without the woman he loves so deeply. But Romeo, as well as Liang Shanbo, the hero in *Butterfly Lovers*, should know that the woman who truly loved him would certainly like to see him live with courage and be able to cheer up even when she was not around. And similarly, Juliet should know that Romeo, if he truly loved her, would not have loved to see her die.

But literature being what it is, the greater the attachment, the greater is deemed the love. I can see that making a great sacrifice, including laying down one's life, to better the life of someone else reflects a great love. But if the loved one had already died, killing oneself is a sacrifice for no good cause. Such literary works may reflect the inherent obsessiveness of uncultivated human nature, but glorifying this kind of love as great has distorted the meaning of greatness and indirectly encouraged many young people to do silly things if for some reason they could not wed or keep their loved ones with themselves.

Obsessions: sunk costs and past glory

In economics there is a very useful concept called *sunk costs*. Sunk costs are spent and cannot be recovered. Economists advise that sunk costs should not be considered at all in decision making. Decision making should be based on the costs and benefits *arising from* a decision. There is a lot of wisdom in this concept, because it advises us that, rather than being bogged down by the past, we should focus on the here and now. In so far as we make the best decision possible now, we will realise the best that is possible. Being obsessed by sunk costs would affect our ability to make the best decision now.

Going back to romantic love, which by definition includes a strong sense of attachment, many couples when they have to break up cannot totally leave the episode behind. This obsession very much reflects a mental inertia. Because we are so used to something we are psychologically not prepared for any change. But this is really silly because there is nothing you can do to salvage anything, if it is truly a *sunk cost*. Once the nature of a sunk cost has been recognised, therefore, the best strategy is always to leave it totally behind.

Another example of a sunk cost is years spent in acquiring a skill. Suppose that skill has now become obsolete, or alternatively suppose some opportunity arises that offers you new possibilities that are very attractive and that are entirely within reach. The wise person would forget about the sunk cost altogether. After all, it is the future that counts. Being bogged down by things in the past limits 'self-actualisation'.

Related to 'sunk costs' is 'past glory'. Some very successful enterprises are bogged down by past glories and complacency, and are not able to evolve with the times. The stories of Wang Computers, Xerox and Kodak are prime examples. One key and fatal decision was founder Dr. Wang's insistence that his son, Fred Wang, should succeed him. Fred Wang was not able to retain the key staff in charge of research and development, and was too immersed in Wang Computers' past glory to understand the challenges that faced the company. The fall of Xerox from grace and its return are particularly illuminating. G. Richard Thoman was hired from IBM in 1997 to become president and chief operating officer at Xerox by then-CEO Paul A. Allaire. But Allaire became board chairman and never really gave Thoman a free hand to run the company, and so the board had too many insiders scared of change and unable to face the challenges of the fast-changing world of technology. In the end, it took the shrewd leadership of a woman, Ann Mulcahy, to bring the company back from the brink of bankruptcy. When shareholders petitioned to cut research and development she would not budge. Instead, she found other ways to cut costs, including the sale of half the stake held in Fuji Xerox, considered to be the company's jewel in the crown. She made hard decisions, eliminating a total of 28,000 jobs in a company with just over 30,000 employees. With wisdom and fortitude, she transformed the company.[4]

The story of Eastman Kodak is even more striking as an example of a company basking in past glory and failing to meet the challenges of new times. Kodak had long prospered on the 'razor-blade' business model by selling cameras cheaply while making huge profits on films. The time-tested model, unfortunately, rendered the company totally unprepared for new times, to the extent that it actually lost its core business to its own invention – the digital camera. But 'instead of marketing the new technology, the company held back for fear of hurting its lucrative film business, even after digital products were reshaping the market'.[5] Thus Kodak's demise is a classic case of hanging on to the past, and losing the future.

Obsession as cause for lack of resilience and for unforgivingness

Obsession with the disappointing results of a particular incident is why many people lack resilience. Instead of learning from the incident and looking forward to doing better next time, they tend to blame themselves, someone else, or bad luck, and cannot control their emotions. They cannot forgive themselves, nor can they forgive others, for the incident. They fail to understand that what has happened has happened. They fail to understand that if there was a cost to pay, it was a sunk cost, and nothing can be done to salvage it. The longer they let their emotions rule them, the more difficult it will be for them to be on the way again. So instead of saving what has already been lost, they are losing even more.

Resilient people will limit their losses by preventing their emotions from blocking their way to future success. They also reflect on the incident and thus try to learn as much as possible from the experience. In this way they grow stronger, and stand ready to meet the next challenge.

Fortitude appears to be the least important factor from regressions using the LIFE formula. The coefficient ranges from one-third to one-half of the size for Engagement, but Fortitude is really important at crucial times. Before one meets a setback, Fortitude does not play any role. This is why Fortitude appears not to be as important as the other LIFE variables. But when there is a setback, the resilient person survives and becomes stronger, while the one who does not pass the test collapses.

Those who 'forgive and forget' are not bogged down by a painful experience and can move on to take advantage of other opportunities that life offers. Those who have an unforgiving will, on the other hand, miss out what life can offer. This is a key reason why happier people tend to be more successful.

Conclusions: transcendence versus obsessions

Life has to be viewed in its entirety in order to be understood. We would be groping in the dark if we did not attempt to see the 'big picture'. We would never get the fulfilment that is possible. Making the most out of our lives, we must not allow obsessions of any kind to hold us up. Life is like a big picture with bright spots and shadows, which would not make much sense when viewed in isolation. Only when we succeed in transcending the here and now, and take life in its entirety, can we avoid being overjoyed at success and losing heart at frustration or failure. Failing to do so, however, will inevitably lead to greater suffering under the laws of life.

Notes

1 Thaler (1980) coined the term *endowment effect*. Tversky and Kahneman (1991) attributed this result to 'loss aversion'. By explaining the endowment effect by loss aversion they implicitly agree that having to give up something already owned produces a mental bad. To the extent that the mental bad is real, the claim that the endowment effect reflects that people are not rational is invalid.
2 It has been noted that envy is really distinct from jealousy. Jealousy is, in comparison, much more negative. A highly jealous person would destroy what others have achieved, while an envious person would work harder to achieve what others have

achieved. From that perspective, perhaps jealousy should replace envy in this context. See www.wisegeek.com/what-is-the-difference-between-jealousy-and-envy.htm.
3 Fromm, Erich (1964) *The Heart of Man*, Harper & Row.
4 See: www.usnews.com/news/best-leaders/articles/2008/11/19/americas-best-leaders-anne-mulcahy-xerox-ceo
5 'Kodak Failed By Asking The Wrong Marketing Question,' in Forbes, 23 Janury 2012. www.forbes.com/sites/avidan/2012/01/23/kodak-failed-by-asking-the-wrong-marketing-question/

Chapter 9

Fortitude

Introduction

Fortitude is just another word for *resilience*. When things are going smoothly fortitude is not needed and even forgotten, and so Fortitude does not appear to carry a big coefficient in the regression of happiness against the LIFE variables. But it is really important, because most likely each of us will go through some tough times through life. When times are tough the one who perseveres will emerge from the difficulties stronger, wiser and happier, whereas the one who gives up and can't muster the courage to bounce back rarely recovers.

What is the key to resilience? Why are some people so strong that apparently they can survive each time, no matter how tough things become, while others seem to be easily blown away?

One of the keys is a strong 'faith' in life and a belief that after the winter there will be spring. You keep telling yourself that you will tough it out, no matter what. You keep telling yourself that you need to always be ready for the opportunity to rebound when it come. You keep telling yourself that you will not be beaten. Because the goal is so much valued, it is worth the fight and the patience and the hard work.

Fortitude is therefore predicated on a strong sense of purpose. Fortitude, however, does not come automatically once one has a strong sense of purpose. It has to be nurtured, so that one gains strength by first overcoming smaller adversities and then learning to overcome bigger ones. 'Faith in life' is therefore a *mental capital* that needs to be accumulated through *investment*. Being disappointed and frustrated from time to time in smaller ways is actually a blessing in disguise, because only in this way can we develop our inner strength, so we can face bigger adversities.

Building resilience is a great investment because it brings great returns in terms of happiness and a more fulfilling life, which is the return that really matters. This faith is moreover not at all an empty faith. It is based, in part, on the observation in the laws of nature that even the worst storm will pass, and that in the darkness of the night dawn always awaits, and in part, on the life skills that one has accumulated over the years. These skills can be summarised in the term 'self-efficacy'. Along with resilience, hope and optimism, it is an aspect of 'psychological capital' that psychologists have been talking about since the early 1990s. They are actually all related to one another, and they make all the difference between success[1] and failure in life.

Hard work, patience and seeing the big picture

Those who lose faith and collapse in adversity are often too focused on the difficulties of the moment to remember that life makes sense only when looked at in its entirety, and not in segments. If they are able to take a longer-term view, they will realise the importance of patience. If times are really rough, and fighting does not stand much chance of success, the best strategy may well be to conserve your energy and wait, meanwhile remembering your longer-term goal. Trying to fight a big storm recklessly is not the spirit of Fortitude, and it may even constitute a misuse of the precious energy that we still have. The spirit of Fortitude is to survive and to stage a fight only when there is a fighting chance.

Seeing the big picture will tell us that there is value in what you are doing, even when you are conserving your energy. Doing the best you can within the constraints is the spirit of economics, and that coincides with the spirit of Fortitude.

The rise of Jeremy Lin to fame is a case in point. He had suffered many bad turns before, having been undrafted and then cut by two different National Basketball Association teams. He was about to be cut by a third team, when his chance came. With major players suffering from injuries and unable to play, the Knicks had to play him, and Lin seized the opportunity to put up a stunning show.

Jeremy's rise to stardom is not based on good luck. If he had not kept up his skills at top levels through hard work, the chance would have just been a non-event. Instead of complaining about his bad luck he used his precious energy to prepare himself for the golden chance. When the chance eventually came he made the best use of it.

Jeremy cited from the Bible: 'suffering produces character, and character produces hope, and hope does not disappoint us'. When the hard work bears fruit, the fruit is that much sweeter.

Eric Jackson, writing in Forbes,[2] summarised the lessons to be learnt from the Jeremy Lin story in ten points:

1 *Believe in yourself when no one else does.* This belief has to be based on hard work and a strong dedication to your goal. Without the hard work it is not possible to build up the self-confidence. Thus during the time of patiently waiting we still need to work hard to prepare for the moment of truth.
2 *Seize the opportunity when it comes up.* Opportunities come and go. We need to watch out for opportunities as they come. Some opportunities may appear once in a lifetime. Thus always being well prepared is important.
3 *Your family will always be there for you, so be there for them.* The knowledge that your family members are behind you is often a strong boost to morale.

4 *Find the system that works for your style.* This is simply: 'Be yourself; do the best you are at.' This corresponds to comparative advantage in economics. Everybody has some comparative advantage.
5 *Don't overlook talent that might exist around you today on your team.* Too many people dismiss the talent that is available and within their easy reach.
6 *People will love you for being an original, not trying to be someone else.* Again, this is 'Be yourself.' We are all unique and valuable in special ways. We need to discover the potential within ourselves.
7 *Stay humble.* Humility is the precondition for improvement and particularly for personal growth. Only with humility can we learn and accumulate mental capital.
8 *When you make others around you look good, they will love you forever.* Offer others support when they need it, and you will be offered support when you need it.
9 *Never forget about the importance of luck or fate in life.* Gratitude attracts support from others and makes you strong.
10 *Work your butt off.* Hard work is indispensable.

The benefits of adversity

Through history, and across different cultures and countries, there have been many amazing characters who have overcome drawbacks that most would consider tragic, and lived a truly rich, fulfilling life, and thus taught us a great lesson about life.

The story of Hirotada Ototake in Japan is truly inspiring. He was born in 1976 with a congenital condition that left him with almost no arms or legs. Many parents would have abandoned him, and most people would not expect much of a future for him. But he nevertheless learnt to overcome many of the obstacles that he was born with, to participate actively in sports and in academic pursuits, and got into the prestigious Wasada University. His self-portrait story, *No One's Perfect* (2003), described his personal struggle and sold over 4,500,000 copies. He admitted that disabilities were of course not an asset, and that he was not always accepted by others, but rather than shying away from the challenge, he mustered all the strength and ability he could, and managed to convince the world that a strong will and the spirit of never giving up will make a big difference. After publishing his best-seller autobiography, Ototake became a successful sports journalist. In 2007, he took a job as a primary school teacher in Tokyo.

Did the disability ever become an asset to Ototake? In one sense. Without his almost crushing disability, he would not have been able to demonstrate to the world that the human will can be so strong and that a strong will can make such a difference.

The story, as told in *No One's Perfect* left one blogger 'decidedly on edge' for the apparent lack of agony.

> Are we to believe in all his twenty-five years he has never had even one dark night of the soul—wondering, Why me? . . . if Oto is completely happy, then he is either one in a million, or he is a saint.[3]

As a human being, I would not doubt that Ototake had moments of agonising, but the important thing is that he did not let those moments bog him down. He would not let his mind keep dwelling on what he could not do but instead he kept looking for opportunities to make the best use of what he could do.

Ototake's story is not really an accident. It testifies to the unbelievable power within each soul, if only we do not give up. This is not to say that fortitude can make us immortal. Randy Pausch died in the end, but he was never defeated. Randy Pausch is the famous Carnegie Mellon University (CMU) professor whose 'Last Lecture' inspired people around the world as much as Ototake. The stories of Ototake and Pausch tell us that there is life is worth living after all, despite all the adversity.

Pausch delivered his 'Last Lecture', titled *Really Achieving Your Childhood Dreams*, at CMU on 18 September 2007. Like Ototake, Pausch showed his humanity and an unfailing faith in, and deep respect for, life. He was loving, humorous and upbeat, despite the fact that an earlier attempt to arrest his cancerous cells had failed. He capitalised on his otherwise tragic illness in the prime of his life to teach his students and the world that a passion for life and treasuring the valuable time that we have when we are alive are what it takes to live a fulfilling life. A book expanding on the theme of the Last Lecture and carrying the same title has been translated into 46 languages. Spending more than 85 weeks on *The New York Times* bestseller list, the book sold more than 4.5 million copies in print in the United.States alone (Pausch and Zaslow, 2008).

Yet another story along the same theme is about a Chinese teacher from Taiwan. Born in a poor family, Zheng Fengxi (1943–1975)[4] had two deformed legs from birth: below the kneecap his right leg was like a wriggling snake, and his left leg was like a thin twig, with the foot inverted downside up. He was given up at the tender age of 6 by his parents, who figured his life would be better under the care of an elderly man, Mr Zhao, who sold traditional Chinese medicine in the streets while offering a monkey show. But he and the elderly man were harassed by gangs, and he got separated from Zhao. He was fortunately picked up by a kind lady who took good care of him for just over a month until he was eventually reunited with his parents. But life continued to be very difficult. How was it, then, possible for a little boy handicapped and without formal schooling up until age 10, to progress all the way to law school?

He described the story thus (Zheng Fengxi, 1984):

> One day, it was the first day of school for my neighbor. He asked me if I would like to go to school with him for some fun and promised to take me on his back. Without a thought I said 'Sure!' And I went straight home to change for better looking clothing . . .

It was morning assembly. A teacher by the name of Wu Li-qing came over and asked for my name and whether I would like to go to school. I told her everything about how I dreamed for going to school. She said I was quite smart, then wrote five phonetic symbols on the board, and read them out for me. This was too easy for me! I mastered them almost immediately. Then she added ten more phonetic symbols, and I still mastered them quickly. Within 30 minutes I had learnt all the phonetic symbols in Mandarin. She was so surprised that she said, 'You are a genius. If you work hard, you will have a great future. Today is the first day in the school term. Will you register to enroll in our school?' I nodded.

When I went to school the first time on my own, I picked up my spirit, ignored the pain of crawling to school, ignored the dishonor associated with crawling, ignored the shame, ignored the possible jibes from onlookers. I was too excited to care, and I confidently went through the gates of the school, to open up a long page of studying at school.

His autobiography *A Boat in a Restless Ocean* (Zheng Fengxi, 1984) was written after he got married, and when he was working as a teacher in a high school. The book had at least 12 reprints (mine was the 12th). His story inspired many, with a TV serial drama and a film further spreading his philosophy of positive living. He left two daughters when he died of liver cancer at the age of 31. In Taiwan today the Zheng Fengxi Education Foundation is still in operation, offering hope and help to many.

Adversity often implies loss. But fortitude would have us focus not on what we have lost but instead on what we still have, and there is usually something to be gained against every loss. Adversity teaches us not to take what we currently have for granted, and often makes us stronger and thus better prepared for the next adversity. If we value what we still have and learn to do the best with what we still have, we have fulfilled our duties. On the other hand, if we keep mourning over what we have already lost – a bygone and a sunk cost – and fail to make the best use of what is still within our control, that would be really foolish.

Limiting losses

I have read several articles in newspaper columns suggesting that positive psychology is a fad or a 'religion'. The authors of the columns cannot accept that real people can take a positive attitude in times of misfortune, as advised by positive psychologists. If the misfortune is real, why should we not be aggrieved over it?

Actually, positive psychologists never advise that we should pretend that the misfortune never happened. It is also perfectly natural and fine for us to express our grief and other 'negative emotions' like sadness and anger. But these 'negative emotions' are not really negative emotions if they are prevented from becoming destructive. Positive psychology recognises the losses and the misfortunes as such but advises that we limit the losses to what have already been incurred. Limiting the losses means that, while expressing sadness, grief and anger is fine, we do not dwell on the foregone losses and never allow our sense of loss to overwhelm and shatter our lives.

For example, suppose we are caught in an accident and have to face the fact that a leg has to be amputated. This is a physical loss that we have to recognise. The best strategy is clearly, having recognised this fact, learning to cope with it rather than being upset over it for an extended period of time. The positive psychologist would advise that it is perfectly fine to cry for a day or two, but rather silly to keep crying for a year instead of learning to cope with the situation.

Similarly, if we have been robbed or have lost money on the stock market, losing sleep over it will not help. Allowing the sense of loss to damage our life further is adding another loss on top of the loss that has already taken place. Bygones are bygones. Sunk losses cannot be reversed.

Fortitude thus is not only driven by a strong sense of purpose, but is also helped by the wisdom to limit losses.

Dealing with unreasonable people

From time to time the chances are that we will encounter unreasonable people who might make life very difficult for us. If we bump into these unreasonable people in the street it is not so difficult to dismiss them by ignoring them and moving on. If, however, they occupy a certain position, such as when they are your boss, your subordinate, your colleague or your client, then you will have to deal with them. They can be manipulative and may want to exploit the situation to their advantage; they may just like bullying people; they may be stubborn and do not know any better.

Let us consider some of the advice that spiritual masters in the past have given. From the *Daodejing*, we have:

> If people are good, I shall be good to them. If people are not good, I shall also be good to them. This way I am really good. If people are truthful, I shall be truthful to them. If people are not truthful, I shall also be truthful to them. This way I am really truthful.[5]

From the Gospel According to St Matthew (5:39): 'But I say unto you, That you resist not evil: but whosoever shall smite you on your right cheek, turn to him the other also.'

Most people would wonder: what is the sense of this? The message is not to be taken literally, but simply underscores the need not to harbour hatred or anger against an unreasonable person. There is a related story from the Buddhist tradition which goes like this. One day an angry man came to Buddha (Buddha means 'the all-enlightened one'). This man was a spiritual teacher himself, but he was angry with the Buddha for challenging his ideas and beliefs and taking students from him. Instead of exchanging wrathful words with him, the Buddha went on his way peacefully. The angry man grabbed some dirt from the ground and threw the earth at him. At this time a strong wind blew in the opposite direction and the earth, instead of hitting the Buddha, landed on the angry man, who was shaken with awe. Thence the Buddha said to him: 'If someone without a good cause uses malicious language and insults an upright person, the insult would only revert to him, just like the dirt that is thrown out coming back to defile him.' On another similar occasion, the Buddha responded to an angry and abusive challenger by asking him if he sometimes entertained friends with a sumptuous meal. Upon a positive response Buddha asked him: 'What would you do with the food if it is not eaten?' The man responded: 'I shall have to take it back.' Buddha then said: 'I have not eaten any of the abusive words you have served me. So you will have to take them back. If I had exchanged similar abusive words with you we would be like people having meals together.'[6]

The spirit of these three pieces of advice from three different ancient sources is exactly the same. You do what you should and maintain your stand, your composure and your integrity. With people who do not reason, you do not argue with them ('having meals of abusive words together with the unreasonable people') or avenge their wrongs. Other people's wrongdoing does not justify our own wrongdoing. As long as we do what we believe is the right thing to do we will live in good conscience.

It is important to distinguish between things that are within our control and things that are beyond our control. What we think and what we do are within our control, so our duty and primary responsibility is simply to make the decisions consistent with our common long-term good. Let other people straighten out their own lives, but we have to straighten out ours. When we do so, there is a chance that the others will eventually change their ways. Human dynamics is such that a philosophy of 'an eye for an eye, a tooth for a tooth' would never bring enduring peace.[7]

Conclusions

Professor Yew-kwang Ng used to ask the audience in public lectures and in class if they thought it was better to be severely disabled (losing both legs or both eyes) or to be killed in an accident. He found that shows of hands indicated that those who were in favour of being killed typically outnumbered those in favour of being severely handicapped by about 2–3 to 1. Professor Ng would then tell them, 'your preferences are incorrect!' Citing Brickman *et al.* (1978), he pointed out that studies show that quadriplegics are only slightly less happy than healthy people. 'After a period of adjustment, the happiness levels of seriously disabled accident victims are [typically] restored to levels close to the pre-accident levels' (Ng and Ng, 2000). The resilience of people, if they give themselves the chance to test it, often goes beyond what they believe! How sad it is, then, to see people committing suicide in the face of some adversity that they thought was grave but that actually would not hurt that much over the long run.

Like Love and Insight, Fortitude can be cultivated. It is through learning to overcome smaller adversities that we gradually learn to overcome bigger adversities. But the courage to face and overcome adversities is always driven by a strong sense of purpose, particularly Love. When such a strong sense of purpose has been identified, achieving the purpose becomes much bigger than serving one's ego. When the ego itself is forgotten, Fortitude emerges, and it grows into a gigantic force.

People who are really strong have their minds set on higher things and on longer-term goals than most people ever dream of. Because they see *success* as realising the best that is possible within the constraints that they face, they are not defeated by short-term reversals. They could lose a battle, but they would never admit defeat. As long as they keep their eyes on their longer-term goals and keep fighting, they will indeed never lose the war. Rather than losing the war, because they make sure that each day of their lives brings them closer to their goals, their lives are truly successful. Their perseverance, truthfulness and passionate endeavours testify to the most valuable qualities known to humanity. Whichever day their life journeys end, they will have lived a meaningful, fulfilling life.

Notes

1 In this book 'success' always refers to being able to realise fully the potential in life. More on this will be discussed in the last chapter.
2 Available online at: www.forbes.com/sites/ericjackson/2012/02/11/9-lessons-jeremy-lin-can-teach-us-before-we-go-to-work-monday-morning/ (accessed 17 June 2013).
3 The blog was signed by L. W. Milam. See: www.ralphmag.org/AG/ototake.html.
4 Wade-Giles, 'Cheng Feng-Hsi.'
5 www.ln.edu.hk/econ/staff/daodejing%2822%20August%202002%29.pdf: Chapter 49.
6 Stories 39 and 40 in *A Hundred Stories about the Buddha*, downloadable from: www.ln.edu.hk/econ/staff/100stories.pdf.
7 Interested readers may also visit: www.psychologytoday.com/blog/prescriptions-life/201201/dont-try-reason-unreasonable-people.

Chapter 10

Engagement
Living with a purpose

Introduction

Traditionally, economists assume that individuals maximise 'utility'. Rational decision makers are assumed to maximise the 'discounted value' of utility over the rest of their lifetime. This perspective prompts the question: Does this mean maximising utility is the purpose of living?

This sounds very mundane, but it need not be. 'Utility' is just a term referring to the value associated with anything that is considered desirable. If helping others is deemed desirable, then you can refer to the utility of helping others. If finding peace is deemed desirable, you may also refer to the utility of finding peace. Economists assume that rational beings seek utility. This is just their methodology, and carries no value judgement as to the worthiness of their pursuits. Granted this, can we regard seeking utility as the purpose of living?

Seeking utility or happiness would sound alien to Kant's characterisation of the purpose of living, even though he does not exactly decry happiness as such. To him, there is a *categorical imperative* for us to 'act only according to that maxim whereby [we] can, at the same time, will that it should become a universal law' (Kant, 1964). This is the *call of duty*: doing something that is worthy entirely for its own sake and not as a means to something desired.[1]

It may be surprising to note that even following the *call of duty* can be reconciled with utility maximisation!

Following the call of duty does not free us from having to make choices. Choices are unavoidable in real life, and whenever we make a choice, we have to weigh one choice against another one according to some value metrics in order to make the best choice. Doctors following their call of duty in saving lives sometimes have to decide whether to save A's life or B's life. A calculated choice implies maximisation of 'utility.'

Thus we all have some kind of *value metrics*. The value metrics that we adopt will guide our lives. So it is important to talk about value metrics.

Ends, instrumental targets and means

It is natural that our value metrics change in the course of our life cycle. As a child the key value metrics could be having fun. As a student facing competitive examinations the key value metrics would likely be high grades. As an adolescent the key value metrics could be finding an ideal boyfriend or girlfriend. As a job seeker it could be a high-paying job or a job that offers a good career path. As a company executive it could be promotion, or in the case of a very senior executive, profit maximisation of the firm. As a competitive athlete it could be winning a gold medal. As a parent, the key value metrics are likely to be bringing up a happy and 'successful' child who will excel in studies and then in a career.

Whatever we pursue, having some target makes our lives much more interesting and meaningful. Over the long run, it does not really matter much what we choose to pursue, as long as we follow our hearts. Even in pursuing a career, different careers may offer totally different material rewards and opportunities. There is so much uncertainty that one can never know if one has made the best decision. But choosing a career that does not fit with your personality and for which you do not feel much excitement is most probably a serious mistake.

Whatever goals we have chosen, as we work toward them, we develop certain skills, some of which will prove useful for us later on in life. Yet all of these goals are really merely intermediate targets. In a sense they are all a means to an end rather than the ends themselves.

They are all means to an end because as we pursue these intermediate goals we become more focused and then can perform better, with the result that we stand a far better chance of realising our potential.

None of these intermediate goals should be considered as the ends themselves, because the final goal must be realising the best within our reach, i.e., our full potential for happiness.[2] This is the 'categorical imperative' for all of us. Making money is important, but only in so far as it allows us to survive, and to procure the means for having the most fulfilling life. If we pursue greater wealth at the expense of a more fulfilling life, we become slaves to the money that we pursued. Similarly, if we pursue a career at the expense of a more fulfilling life, we become slaves to the career that we pursue. And we can substitute any of the intermediate goals in this sentence, to underscore the fact that, after all, it is achieving a more fulfilling life that should be the final goal.

That is why it is heart-breaking to see students killing themselves for not being able to meet demands from their school or from the education system, whether imaginary or otherwise. After all, education is supposed to be for their benefit. When instead of benefiting from their education students feel helpless or worthless under its weight, the education must have gone wrong. Education is only a means towards achieving a better life. But when, instead of helping students discover a more worthy life, education drives them to suicide, education can be said to have failed in its mission.

Helping students to see the distinction between means and ends and to know that life is more important than anything else must be central to the mission of education. This is the duty of educators, just as realising each person's full potential that life offers for happiness is the duty of each person, to use Kant's terminology.

It is instructive for us to ask why people confuse means with ends, and this brings us back to the discussion about mental goods and bads. It is no use telling a student that passing an examination is not the most important thing on earth, when all the signs are that passing an examination and getting good grades is super-important. Where and what are these signs? You can see them in the principal's speeches; you can see them in the special sessions that teachers arrange for students after class; you can see the extent to which the timetable is structured; you can see them in conversations among students. When high performers are honoured and poor performers are shamed, students will feel the pressure. Students need to learn that not doing as well in examinations is not such a big deal, although doing the best they can, while maintaining a good work–life balance, is important. We all need to learn the happiness formula, Love, Insight, Fortitude and Engagement, and a truly engaged life with these guiding principles is much more important than merely talking about them.

Learning through thick and thin

The key to purposive living is not only to live with a purpose on some days, but to live fully and passionately with a purpose every day. After all, each day is as precious as any other day in our life. Each day deserves to be used to serve our final purpose, which must be discovering and realising the potential within ourselves. 'A day truly lived is a day truly gained.' Consider the following perspective (Ho, 2011a):

> Whether the day appears to go in one's favor or against one's favor,
> With the right attitude, in the end it will be a good day:
> Because it tests out your sense of equanimity, which if underdeveloped,
> points to more spiritual work;
> Because it takes the totality of life,
> with favorable and unfavorable days combined,
> to enrich and feed one's spiritual life.
>
> Witness the Song of the Truthful Mind.[3]
> Master Sengcan maintains that giving up the idea of favorable and unfavorable
> Leads one naturally to the Supreme.
> For it is said:
>
> 'Before I began my spiritual enterprise
> I saw mountains as mountains, and rivers as rivers.
> When I began my spiritual practice,
> Mountains were no longer mountains,
> And rivers no longer rivers.

When I fulfilled my spiritual endeavor,
Mountains were mountains again, and rivers again rivers.'

It is always attitudes that erred,
Never the external world ('mountains and rivers')
The uninitiated never notice the erring.
The to-be initiated notice the erring, but try to find reality from the outside.
The wise dispel their own biased views, and see reality for what it is.

It is inevitable that some of the days in our life appear to be favourable while some other days appear to be unfavourable, in terms of the intermediate goals that we have chosen for ourselves, or simply in terms of our day-to-day functions. You could make a serious mistake at work, flunk a test, break up with your girlfriend, fall sick, or otherwise run into bad luck of all kinds. Rather than simply dismissing these as bad days, taking a positive attitude could allow us to learn from our experiences.

We have maintained that building up mental capital is not an easy task. It requires much effort and discipline. Then we will gradually build habits that will benefit us. These habits will become part of us (Wood and Neal, 2007). Of these habits the most important are mental: a habit of reflecting, a habit of facing adversity with calm, a habit of organising ourselves to meet challenges, a habit of fearlessness, and a habit of not getting angry and losing control when we are frustrated. It is 'through thick and thin' that we gradually build up our mental capital. It is through thick and thin that people get to know what love is, and learn to acquire wisdom, and learn to stay calm in the face of an adversity. Taking each day of living as a day to uplift oneself spiritually is engagement.

The place of music, entertainment and recreation

Living with a purpose does not mean that the entire day has to be devoted to the identified purpose. There is a need for recreational activities and for entertainment, and particularly for music. When these activities are in the right amounts they are not distractions. Not only do they not distract us from our central activities, but they also energise our lives and enhance our work (Achor, 2010). Still, however, the concept of optimality comes in. In small amounts they bring positive marginal benefits in terms of contributing to the purpose. When the amounts are sufficiently big, the marginal benefits will decline eventually to zero and then fall into the negative zone.

While many activities are considered by most people to be recreational or for entertainment, they could be careers for others. We can manifest our life potentials in a myriad of ways, and artists, in particular, discover and manifest their life potential through artistic expression. Depending on the nature of these activities to the person undertaking them, the optimal amount varies from person to person. Only each individual person can tell if he has had enough.

Mindfulness

True engagement requires mindfulness. That means that the mind has to be disciplined to focus on the task at hand. It means whatever you choose to do, you have to do it wholeheartedly.

Examples to illustrate the principle are easy to find. When a student is attending class, but he allows his mind to wander, that cannot be an effective way of using his time. When someone has migrated from his homeland to a new country, he needs to take his newly adopted country as his home, and be involved in the community and the local life, if he is to live well. If he keeps thinking about his homeland, that cannot be an effective way of spending his life. In a sense, an immigrant who cannot be 'engaged' in activities in the newly adopted country is likely to be wasting his precious life.

Mindfulness and full engagement in a task that has been taken up are not at all easy to achieve. This is because the mind has a habit of wandering away. Those who do meditation will know this very well. For a simple task like watching and counting the breath in and out, almost everyone will find that is awfully difficult to do. Because the mind is so difficult to control, many people are prone to doing silly things without being fully aware of the silliness of the things that they do. By the time they realise, it could be too late, because they will have to live with the consequences, which can be very unpleasant.

Someone who has so disciplined his mind that he can focus his mind easily can do much more than others who cannot. Someone whose mind is out of focus most of the time will let opportunities go past, and will have decisions made by default rather than deliberately.

Mindfulness is particularly important to help us guard against silly, momentary decisions and behaviour that we could regret for life. Sometimes, just a flash of the mind could lead us to misbehave, and the consequences can be very serious. Not being mindful means that we may just not be aware of the dangers of the acts that we may do. There was a case in Hong Kong involving a very promising doctor who had just got his qualifications to work as a physician. But he was convicted of sexually assaulting a patient. With the criminal conviction, his loss is huge. On hindsight, the sexual assault really does not make sense, reflecting a lack of control and a lack of mindfulness. Only when we are mindful and alert can we stop the mind's unbridled adventures from playing havoc with our lives.

To get a glimpse into the mind's unbridled adventures, we may do a very simple exercise, which is sitting down and counting the breath. Each cycle of inhale and exhale will be counted once. Breathe naturally, and just watch the breath and count. After counting to ten, repeat the counting and start with one again. You will find that this apparently simple thing is actually very difficult to do. Focusing the mind on the breath and not losing count is very difficult, because in no time all kinds of thoughts arise, and they interrupt the count. It takes a lot of training just to be able to keep track of the number and not to let the mind wander.

Conclusions

Life is a journey. A journey with a purpose is usually a more interesting journey. Making a journey with curiosity and zeal is always a more fruitful journey than making one in which you merely follow what others do. Different people have different goals in life, and that is just fine. It takes work and effort to achieve any goal. But strangely, most goals in life are intermediate goals, and are more in the nature of an instrument than a destination. Yet goals are very important, for they give us drive and provide us meaning. Which intermediate goal we choose is not nearly as important as simply following our heart: for living in conflict with our nature is very depressing. Because the world is uncertain, you may never know if a particular choice was the best choice at the time. Interestingly, however, it does not matter that much over the long run. As we grow older, moreover, many begin to realise that many of the goals that had been important before are not really that important. What is more important is making sense of our experience. Interestingly, with the right attitude – which is just an open and humble attitude — every day of our lives can be just as inspiring.

This is what Diener and Diener have to say about some of the common goals that people dream about:

> Happiness . . . is a process, not a destination. Just as Cinderella's life did not end with her royal wedding, your emotional bliss is not complete once you have obtained some important goal. Life goes on, and even those great circumstances you achieve will not ensure you lasting happiness. For one thing, bad things can happen even to beautiful young princesses. But even if Cinderella's life encountered few bumps on the fairyland road, she might have grown bored with the wonderful circumstances surrounding her, and needed new aims and activities to add zest to her life.

Engagement means an active life devoted to a purpose, and there is no greater purpose than making the most out of our lives. Manifestation of this can be in a myriad of ways, but living fully always requires paying respect to every experience and every day of our lives. To use Kant's terminology, our 'categorical imperative' and first duty is to discover and realise the potential that life affords us. Following this call of duty is to follow the *laws of nature*, and without explicitly pursuing happiness, one will find a life of fulfilment.

The pursuit (written on a flight from Toronto to Detroit, 3 June 2006)

> People through the ages have been seeking:
> Some seek gratification of the senses;
> Some seek honor, others power;
> Some seek wealth, others knowledge and truth;
> Some seek excitement, others calm;
> Some seek friendship and love, others a place in heaven.
> Some seek an inner peace.

The pursuit goes on, the object varies; the reward also varies:
It may be a happiness that comes and goes –
A momentary elation that ebbs into nothing;
Or a happiness that endures –
A lasting joy that resembles an eternal spring:
The momentary happiness gives way to a sense of loss;
The lasting joy makes known the meaning of love.

The pursuit goes on.
As people chase dreams and shadows,
Making foes and friends,
Creating idols and gods,
Making peace and making wars,
Creating chaos and restoring order.
Making history and repeating history,
Some pursue earthly dreams, others lofty ones:
Unfinished dreams left behind by their forefathers,
And passed on to their progeny and others.

Beautiful temples have crumbled,
Mighty castles have turned into shambles.
Mighty rivers continue to run
Washing earth and debris
From great mountains and along the way, to the insatiable sea.
Only the wise have given up the chase:
Rediscovering a peace and wholeness within,
Their spiritual beings grow and mature,
Beyond possession and strife,
Awakening to a fulfilling and timeless life.

Notes

1 Taking an untraditional perspective, Wike (1994) argued that Kant's key propositions are not inimical to happiness having a positive role to play in Kant's ethic.
2 See the introduction chapter in Ng and Ho (2006), where there is a discussion on happiness as a final goal.
3 A translation of the *Xinxin Ming* or *Song of the Truthful Mind* is provided in *Human Spirituality and Happiness* (Ho, 2011a). See also: en.wikipedia.org/wiki/Xinxin_Ming.

Chapter 11

Three happinesses and transcendental happiness

Introduction

These days we hear more and more people preach about the benefits of 'living in the present'.[1] However, this is very difficult to do because, on the one hand, regrets about the past may prove difficult to ignore, while on the other, worries about the future may distract our attention from the present. As a result, we may not be fully engaged in the task at hand. Our performance may decline, and we may fail to get as much out of an episode of our life as we can. Since the present is really the only time when we can make a difference, failing to do the best we can translates to wasting the precious life that we have.

A team of researchers from Princeton University developed a systematic account of 'evaluated time use'. The study, based on a nationwide telephone survey of nearly 4,000 people in the spring and summer of 2006 with the help of the Gallup Organization, tried to collect information on individuals' reported emotional experiences, such as the intensity of pain, happiness, stress, and so forth.[2] Based on this Princeton Affect and Time Survey (PATS), the research team compiled a 'U-index' that measures the proportion of time an individual spends in an unpleasant state. The unpleasant state is defined as an episode in which the maximum rating on any of the negative affect dimensions, such as 'depressed', 'angry' and 'frustrated', is strictly greater than the maximum of rating of the positive affect dimensions, such as 'happy', 'enjoy myself' and 'friendly'.

This approach does offer some advantages, and complements national income accounting in that it offers additional information about wellbeing that national income accounting always ignores. Yet it also assumes that the effects are intrinsically associated with the activity. The fact is that the extent to which an activity is pleasant or unpleasant often depends on the attitude of the person undertaking the activity, and may not really be intrinsic to the activity as such. For example, you may take a taxi to cover a one-mile journey, to save you walking, even when you are not pressed for time. But then people may walk or jog for exercise. There is the story of an official in the Jin period in ancient China by the name of Tao Kan (259–334), who was demoted and semi-exiled to the then remote city of Guangzhou in the south at the displeasure of the emperor. He had nothing much to do, and decided to keep fit by moving 100 bricks from his study to his courtyard in the morning and moving them back to his study in the evening. Certainly moving the bricks is physically very strenuous, as is rock climbing, or even doing a work-out in the gym.

Moreover, as Cutler points out in his chapter in the same conference volume, while the U-index and the evaluated time use approach can measure the utility derived from the activity, 'they are less good at measuring the value of what comes out'. From a more holistic perspective, an activity that may not be as pleasant at the moment – particularly the effort and the sacrifice made – may make the achievement of a goal possible and meaningful. The satisfaction thus derived is for that reason much greater.

Past, present and future

Jeremy Bentham is well known as the father of utilitarianism, and his 'felicific calculus' would have us subtract all the pains and add all the pleasures to get the net gains in terms of utility. But life is really an integral whole, and is much more than the sum of its parts. From this perspective, the past is linked to the present, and the present is linked to the future. In a sense, although a bygone is a bygone in the sense that you cannot go back to the past and remake a decision, what was done in the past unavoidably is reflected in the present, while what we do today will certainly be reflected in the life we will inherit tomorrow.

The past is affecting our life condition today in three ways. First, and this had been discussed before, our past activities led to the accumulation of both positive and negative mental capital. Some people may like to call this 'karma', but whatever you call it, the habits that we have today are affecting our lives. Some of these habits have become so much part of ourselves that they are our personal traits and are very difficult to break. Second, pleasant experiences with other people in the past tend to make us more optimistic and trusting of others, while unpleasant experiences in the past tend to make us more pessimistic and distrustful of others. Third, regrets about something we did wrong in the past often haunt us, while past generosity and kindly acts tend to give us peace of mind, so we are more able to enjoy the pleasures and delights of the here and now.

Because the past can affect our life conditions so much, and because the here and now will become the past, we need to be mindful of our activities today, so we can accumulate positive mental capital.

The future is also affecting our life conditions in several ways. First, we may worry about uncertainty. We are generally more comfortable with what we are familiar with, but are unsure of whether we can cope when something that we are not familiar with happens to us. Second, we may worry about something terrible that may or may not happen to us. For example, during the episode of severe acute respiratory syndrome (SARS) that struck China and the Hong Kong Special Administrative Region and then spread to the rest of the world, many people were terrified, and were afraid of meeting people and of travelling. The airlines had a very difficult time because there were hardly any passengers on most flights. Third, we may look forward to a much brighter future, so we are able to cherish hope even during times of difficulties and great hardship.

It is interesting to note that our happiness *today* is not determined just by what we experience today, but also by past events and experiences, and by the future that has not yet arrived.

We tried to test the 'three happinesses hypothsis', which, to put it simply, states that the past and the future, as much as the present, all have an important bearing on our happiness.

The Centre for Public Policy Studies of Lingnan University in Hong Kong designed three groups of questions to gauge the effects of past, present and future on the happiness of people. Respondents were asked if they agreed or disagreed with the statements below, on a scale of 0 to 10, with 0 being 'most disagree' and 10 being 'most agree'.

Prospective happiness

- I meet each day with excitement and joy.
- I do not usually worry about the future.
- I expect to continue to learn more things in the rest of my life.

Happiness in process

- I enjoy my work/housework.
- I enjoy my time with my family.

Retrospective happiness

- I am pleased with how I have conducted my life.
- I have grown wiser because I am able to learn from my mistakes.

The average scores of each of these three categories are then used as regressors to explain the overall happiness index, which is also on an 11-point scale (0–10). The sample in each year is subdivided into three age groups and the regression separately run. The results are listed in Table 11.1.

It is interesting to note that the weights of both prospective happiness and happiness in process tend to decline with age. This seems to make sense, because as one gains in age, life expectancy declines, and health conditions tend to deteriorate. On the other hand either retrospective happiness remains high or the constant term climbs with age. The constant term may be called *transcendental happiness*: the happiness we achieve when considering our life as a whole, beyond the present, the past and the future.

The movements in LIFE scores, which are available from 2008 and are listed in Table 11.1, indicate that there has been an uptrend in these score in Hong Kong in recent years, and this uptrend mirrors an increase in the happiness index, as shown in Figure 11.1.

Table 11.1 Three happinesses over the life cycle 2008

Age (years) (observations)	21–29 (163)	30–60 (502)	60 or above (94)
Constant	1.322 (2.751)***	1.442 (4.383)***	1.259 (1.582)
Prospective happiness	**0.419** (4.666)***	0.279 (6.389)***	0.228 (2.005)***
Happiness in process	0.37 (4.562)***	0.233 (4.942)***	0.262 (2.365)**
Retrospective happiness	0.036 (0.461)***	**0.293** (5.808)***	**0.353** (3.316)***
R bar square (F-statistic)	0.476 (50.416)***	0.396 (110.794)***	0.393 (21.276)***

Notes
Figures in bold indicate the highest of the 'three happinesses' for the age group.
*** Significant at 1%; ** significant at 5%.

Transcendental happiness

In the happiness surveys conducted by the Centre for Public Policy Studies of Lingnan University, the key question asked to gauge the happiness of the respondent is: 'Taking everything together, how would you rate your overall happiness, if 0 is least happy and 10 is most happy?' The reference to 'overall happiness' is deliberate, and is an attempt to prompt respondents not to report their mood at the moment or 'these days'. It is very common for the key happiness

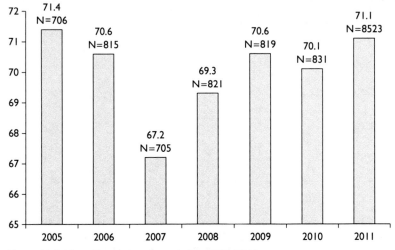

Figure 11.1 Hong Kong's happiness index 2005–2011.

92 Three happinesses and transcendental happiness

question to ask respondents to rate their happiness 'these days'. But 'happiness these days' may be construed of as moods, and these readily change with circumstances, while overall happiness is more 'enduring'. The constant term in the three-happiness equation refers to such transcendental happiness that is based on an evaluation of total life satisfaction beyond retrospective happiness, prospective happiness nor process happiness. It is based on new meanings discovered when life is seen as a whole rather than in parts.

There is an imprecision in language that we need to be aware of. The same words can mean different things to different people, and some words are more prone to conjuring up connotations that other words. Transcendental happiness, as mentioned in the last paragraph, is based on an evaluation of total life satisfaction, but when the term total life satisfaction is mentioned, respondents tend to look at various aspects of their life condition to assess if there are some that they would like to be improved. Thus a blind person, when asked about total life satisfaction, is likely to offer a lower rating than when asked about overall happiness, since a blind person may notwithstanding the blindness be perfectly happy.

While it is true that in some contexts 'happy' and 'satisfied' are used interchangeably, such as in the statement, 'I am happy with the outcome,' when asked about overall happiness, the respondent is likely to distinguish this from overall life satisfaction. A regression of the happiness index against the LIFE scores is found to yield statistically more significant coefficients than a regression of total life satisfaction index on the same variables.(Table 11.2).

Table 11.2 Regression results on happiness versus life satisfaction using 2011 telephone survey from Hong Kong

	Happiness	Total life satisfaction
Love	0.23	0.35
	(3.76)	(1.82)
Insight	0.24	0.44
	(4.07)	(3.05)
Fortitude	0.16	−0.03
	(2.79)	(−0.17)
Engagement	0.09	−0.16
	(1.50)	(−0.37)
Constant term	1.88	2.34
	(3.71)	(3.35)
Observations	723	725
F	31.55	22.99
Probability > F	0.0000	0.0000
R-squared	0.3258	0.0407

t-score in parentheses.

Conclusions

Seligman in his book *Authentic Happiness* had chapters on the past, the present and the future. He recognised the fact that happiness in general is not just based on the 'here and now'. Some people feel miserable because they cannot forget traumatic events in the past or they have some misgivings about how they have been treated unfairly, or because they feel they made a grave mistake in the past. Their here and now is haunted by their past. They therefore cannot be really engaged in the here and now. At the same time, although the future has not yet arrived, the future may be taking its toll on happiness now, as people are worried about it. Alternatively, people may look forward to the future so much that they feel excited and joyful right now.

Studies based on the data from Hong Kong shows that for many people the past has a great impact on their happiness. The effect can be positive or negative. If a person is very satisfied with how he conducted his life in the past, he is more able to accept himself. His self-esteem will be higher, and he may cherish love and other positive emotions that will continue to accompany him for the rest of his life. On the other hand, past regrets, grievances and lack of forgiveness may undermine a person's self-esteem, and he is liable to get angry at small irritations, and may continue to suffer from a sense of guilt.

In general, the past, although it is gone, must have left its mark on a person's general outlook and mental capital. Some of the effects of the past may be retained in the coefficient to the retrospective happiness variable, and some may spill over to the constant term, and become crystallised in the form of 'transcendental happiness'. It is not surprising that, as LIFE scores climbed from 2008 to 2009, the constant term also went up.

Notes

1 An example is easy to find on the internet: www.illuminatedmind.net/2008/02/20/how-to-live-fully-in-the-present/.
2 See Alan Krueger, Daniel Kahneman, David Schkade, Norbert Schwarz, and Arthur Stone, Chapter 1, in Alan B. Krueger (ed.) (2009) *Measuring the Subjective Well-Being of Nations: National Accounts of Time Use and Well-Being*, National Bureau of Economic Research.

Chapter 12

Avoiding regrets and coming to terms with past errors

Introduction

Regrets are a source of unhappiness and stress. When we regret, we recognise that we have made errors in the past. Some of these errors we are really responsible for, in the sense that, with a little more self-control, with an exercise of reasonable judgement, we would not have made those errors. Some of them however were not really our responsibility, in the sense that our best judgement at the moment would have led us to the same decisions, or we simply did not have the information to make an informed choice. But the decision has been made; what has been done has been done.

There are therefore two issues here. First is avoiding true errors. Second is coming to terms with the errors, whether or not we are responsible.

Avoiding true errors

As humans we all make errors. Some errors are obviously much more serious than others. With small errors, the ensuing pain or sorrow is relatively minor, and we readily pick up the pieces and go on our journey of life. With big errors, the ensuing pain or sorrow may be really difficult to swallow. A big error could haunt you for the rest of your life. So it is really important to avoid big errors.

When a truly big error has already been made, we have no choice but to come to terms with it. The best way to deal with it is to limit the losses. I shall deal with this in the next section.

To minimise true errors, we need to know that they fall into several categories.

First is overestimating our ability. We may think we have not drunk that much, and we can manage to drive even after drinking. We may think that our driving skills are very good, and we can harness a newly bought and very powerful sports car. We may think that we will not get addicted to the drug, even though we try it several times. We may get hooked on gambling after losing some money and keep trying our luck to recoup the losses, which then grow bigger and bigger.

Second is mistrusting someone. We may mistrust a business partner or an employee, and then allow them to dictate our fate by giving them too much discretionary power. In a corporate setting, an example is the case of *rogue traders* like Nick Leeson, whose unauthorised trading from his Singapore office led to the fall of Barings Bank in 1995 following a loss of £827 million due to speculative investing in Nikkei Index futures. We may also mistrust a friend whom we have known for a long time but who nevertheless turned out to betray our interest or cheat us of our fortune under various pretences.

Third is falling prey to temptation. There could appear to be a rare and irresistible opportunity to make huge profits, to indulge in a romantic or erotic encounter, or to have access to some 'fast track to success' through illicit dealings. Or we just might lose judgement over an easy opportunity to pocket small benefits.

Fourth is carelessness. A careless mistake could lead to big losses that you could regret for the rest of your life. Related to this is failing to see all the warning signs that were there and that should have prevented you from making the mistake, if only you did not blind yourself somehow.

Fifth is failing to control our emotions. We could be so irritated by even small things that in a fury we might do silly things that we regret later.

Sixth is taking too big a gamble. There are many situations in life when decisions have to be made under uncertainty. Making unnecessary big gambles could lead to regrets.

Seventh is the worst mistake. It is failing to recognise the mistakes we have made, and instead convincing ourselves that it was bad luck rather than we ourselves who caused all the problems.

Eighth is exactly the contrary. It happens when we regret and grieve over a mistake excessively instead of learning from it – more on this in the next section.

There is one thing in common among most of these mistakes. This is the role played by a strong ego. When the strong ego gets the better of us we suppress legitimate questions instead of addressing them. We dismiss the warning signs, assume our judgement could not be wrong, assume our abilities would not fail us, or let our emotions rule over us. The seventh and worst mistake, clearly, is made when the ego wins the game entirely. Such individuals will take all their mistakes to the grave, and will not learn a thing from them. Their precious years would be entirely wasted.

Still, 'to err is human, to forgive divine,' as poet Alexander Pope says. But we should learn from our mistakes and try our best to minimise them. To avoid making or repeating mistakes it is important to recognise them and to be in a state of *mindfulness* at all times, because it takes only a flash of mind for the mistake to be made, often without our even being aware of it.

Coming to terms with past errors: limiting the losses

'To forgive, divine,' so the saying goes. This underscores how difficult it is to forgive. Actually, when we say 'forgive', we really mean 'to forgive and forget'. Here 'forget' is not to forget the lesson learnt, but to forget and thus get relieved of the burden in our hearts. Coming to terms with past errors is making a deal with ourselves not to let the burden bog us down in the rest of our journey through life, whether the errors are ours or others.

Past mistakes are a lost cost. A lost cost is a bygone. Economics teaches us that bygones are bygones, and they should no longer count as a cost in our future decisions. Only when we relieve ourselves of the burden of our past errors can we limit the losses. Otherwise the past mistakes will jeopardise our current and future decisions, while the burden of the memory makes us unhappy. The losses then grow into even bigger losses, and we could waste the rest of our lives.

Coming to terms with past errors requires us to take full responsibility for the consequences while refusing to be bogged down by those consequences. The consequences can be very hard, but trying to run away from them will not help. After all, it is we who made the errors in the first place. Taking full responsibility for the consequences allows us to have peace of mind. We have learnt the lesson, and we have grown. We paid the price, and we must take the benefit of the lesson by growing wiser and stronger, or the price would have been paid in vain.

Coming to terms with past errors means that we may have to go through a really difficult ordeal, which requires Fortitude or resilience. Renowned journalist Mike Wallace was in a depression in 1984 with a libel lawsuit against him from US Army General William Westmoreland for the story 'The Uncounted Enemy: A Vietnam Deception', aired on CBS News. Although the libel suit was eventually dropped, Wallace was so overwhelmed by worries that he attempted suicide. Had he 'succeeded', he would have made a far greater error than any that he had already made. He certainly would not have been able to tell his story, and would not have made such a huge contribution to the world of investigative reporting as he did. Describing that experience, Wallace expressed his gratitude to his fourth wife Mary Yates:

> I was sliding down the slope into a clinical depression. As fall gave way to winter, I sank ever more deeply into that dark and devastating malaise, which was crushing my spirit and even sapping my will to live. Shortly before the New Year, I came perilously close to committing suicide. I probably would have taken the plunge into that abyss had it not been for the love and caring support I received from the woman in my life, who was both an old friend and a new romance . . . The woman I'm referring to was Mary Yates.
>
> (Wallace and Gates, 2005, p. 200)

In that memoir Wallace did not admit to having actually attempted suicide. But in a 2006 interview honouring his retirement as a *60 Minutes* correspondent, Wallace admitted it. While it was sheer luck that he survived the attempt, it was the love and support from his wife that ignited his will to recover. In the end it was his determination to recover that really saved and revived him. Wallace eventually lived to the age of 93, and his life of devotion to his work, particularly after his revival from depression, brought him accolades from all over the world. But the story could easily have been totally different. A momentary lapse of judgment could have ended Wallace's life in 1986. A worthy life would then have been lost.

Errors but really not our errors

Unlike the errors for which we really have to take responsibility for, often times we make errors through no fault of our own, but because of the circumstances, which are really beyond our control. A doctor exercising his best judgement could misdiagnose. A driver could be involved in an accident because of someone else's mistakes. A journalist may do his work professionally and in good conscience, and still get entangled in a libel suit. Sometimes we could even be wrongly accused of something that we have not done. Thanks to the Innocence Project, hundreds of Americans have now been exonerated from serious crimes that had led to an average of 13.5 years in prison. Here are some facts on post-conviction DNA exonerations.

- Total number of DNA exonerations up to 2012: 289
- Number of exonerations since 2000: 222
- Number of exonerated who were serving time on death row: 17
- Average age of exonerees at the time of their wrongful convictions: 27.

Those who were wrongly convicted may have been in the wrong place at the wrong time, and had been misidentified. In some cases they could have been woefully used as scapegoats. The fact is that misfortunes can happen to us. We may be totally innocent, and it is not only the legal system that may have wronged us. Our best friends and our dear ones could have faulted us for something we have not done. I saw horrifying stories when some innocent people had been taken by police for drug trafficking in foreign countries. Corrupt police officers may want to get a bribe from innocent people. The list of possible misfortunes is endless.

To protect ourselves and our dear ones, clearly, it is really important to avoid going to the wrong places at the wrong times. There are places where one could run into trouble more easily than elsewhere. They should be avoided, unless there is a really good reason. Reporters risk their lives reporting from dangerous places, and they deserve our deepest respect. In these cases we pay a price for something we believe in, or something we value. If that is our decision, we will have to be ready to face the consequences. If an unfortunate situation has already happened, it is important not to lose heart. Persevering and trying to look for an opportunity to limit losses and to make the most out of a difficult situation would be the wisest thing to do. Although we cannot count on it, perseverance may well pay off, and in a sense it always pays off. By not losing heart and doing the best we can, regardless of the turnout, we are nevertheless realising our potential to the best of our ability. It is something we can be proud of in the end.

Conclusions

Regrets are a mental bad and a common cause of unhappiness, and they often follow decisions that are bad on hindsight. But regrets are useless, just as unforgiving anger is useless. Both regrets and unforgiving anger will magnify the damage that has already been done. If the error was our own, we should learn from it, and then should congratulate ourselves that we survived, becoming wiser. If the error was others', we should learn to *forgive and forget,* so we can be relieved of the burden that will otherwise spoil our present and undermine our future.

'Forgive' is not the same as allowing a criminal to go unpunished. If a criminal has done someone grave wrongs, he should certainly be held fully responsible and accountable and punished. Deterring crimes by appropriate punishment is a noble goal. Forgiving is simply refusing to let the anger spoil our lives, and does not mean letting a criminal go. Forgiving does mean, however, a wish that the criminal would in his heart recognise his errors and that he would aspire to a new life, not repeating those errors.

Chapter 13

Avoiding worries and coming to terms with an uncertain future and negative emotions

Introduction

We live in an uncertain world, and there are always many unknowns in the future; we can never be sure where dangers are lurking without our knowing. Here is the report of an accident that led to the death of 16 people in Arkansas in June 2010:

> Tragedy strikes Arkansas when flash floods hit the Caddo and Little Missouri rivers that rose by 20 feet overnight. The result was the hikers and campers who were spending the night in tents along the rivers in the isolated Ouachita Mountains were unsuspectingly swept away. It was reported that 16 people had died in flash floods and dozens are missing in Arkansas after flood waters swept through a camp ground. Sadly, many of the the dead reported are children and there are still as many as 20 people still missing after the flash flood.[1]

In 2010 a tourist group was about to leave a parking lot in Manila when a gunman suddenly got into the bus and held them hostage. The incident ended up with eight Hong Kong tourists shot and killed and many others wounded. Should people not visit a foreign country? Hong Kong today (August 2013) still has not lifted the black outbound travel alert for the Philippines.

The fact is that, while we can and should avoid some obvious dangers, we can never be sure if some unforeseen mishaps are awaiting us as we conduct our day-to-day lives. But worries are of absolutely no use. Worries only undermine our welfare and make us less happy.

During the episode of severe acute respiratory syndrome (SARS) attacks in 2002–2003 some 300-plus people died in Hong Kong and globally some 810 deaths were reported from 29 countries. This number is a tiny fraction of fatalities from traffic accidents – in 2009, some 36,000 people died from motor vehicle accidents. But people were so scared that airlines saw their passenger numbers plunge to a tiny fraction of normal. The fear and worries were affecting people's lives even though the vast majority of people never contracted the disease.

Before SARS caught up with us we had already lost our welfare significantly, all because we were worried. Clearly worrying does not help.

Coming to terms with uncertainties

Worrying is not the same as recognising a possible risk. We all need to recognise possible risks, and then try to avert the dangers or to minimise the losses in the event a mishap occurs. But worrying is counterproductive. Rather than goading us into action where action is due, worrying, particularly panicking, prevents us from taking proper action.

There are things that are within our control, and things that are beyond our control. Doing what is necessary and appropriate within our control and not worrying about things that are beyond our control is the best strategy at all times. This, unfortunately for many, is easier said than done.

Here again, *mindfulness* training comes to our aid. The worry creeps back, and keeps creeping back without our being aware of it. With sufficient mindfulness training, when the worry creeps back we know. We can speak to the worry: 'Here you are again. Go away!'

We can tell ourselves positively: Worrying is of no use. My duty and responsibility now are to do whatever is within my control to avert the possibilities of danger and to minimise possible losses. Once I have done this I have done my job. I shall leave it to [my Father in heaven, my fate, whatever]. Whatever comes, I shall take it as it comes.

In all likelihood we will have to do this again and again, until it becomes a habit. Then we shall have accumulated a *mental capital* against worries and *panic attacks*. This is *investing in mental capital*.

Think about an infant. An infant is totally dependent on adults to take care of him. There are so many things that an infant could worry about. If he worried about these possibilities, he would not be able to eat well and to sleep well. An infant's responsibility and duty are therefore simply to eat when it is time to eat, to sleep when it is time to sleep, to have a bowel movement and to urinate as the natural urge comes, and to leave everything else to his parents or other adults.

Here is a poem that might help in mindfulness training to avert worries and panics. Read it slowly, and imagine that it was a friend talking to you. No matter how difficult the situation is, give yourself a break.

Blessed

(26 May 2006, Villa Serbelloni, Bellagio, 6 a.m.)

> Blessed are those who can put down
> The day's worries and concerns . . .
>
> Never mind if it rains or shines tomorrow.
> Never mind if it is right or wrong.
> Never mind if someone is honest or dishonest.
> Never mind if someone understands me or not.
> Never mind if someone means ill or well.
> Never mind.

Forget gains and losses.
Let it be.
Only know that
You are blessed.
Let sleep come naturally.
Let the new day come naturally.

Smile a natural smile.
Let blessings come Nature's way.
For you are always at home,
          wherever you go.

Coming to terms with difficulties and misfortunes

There are times when the situation is really difficult. One indeed can encounter bad luck. And there are times when the consequences of our past mistakes catch up with us. Coming to terms with the difficulties and the misfortunes is recognising them for what they are. Whatever is the reality is something that we will have to face. It is always better to face the consequences than to try to run away from them. If the bad consequences are a result of our past mistakes we will learn from the mistakes, and we will pick up the courage to face the consequences. If the difficulties are a result of bad luck, we will accept the fact that bad luck is

Figure 13.1 'Blessed'. Courtesy S. K. Chan.

sometimes unavoidable, but that it is only part of life. The difficulties will pass, and even though the circumstances are hard, toughing it out will usually bring rewards down the road. There is often a silver lining behind the difficulties, and difficulties do build character.

Coming to terms with negative emotions

Negative emotions are part of us, and we have to overcome them. This is true of everyone, since everyone has negative emotions. Overcoming them is a challenge, and is not going to be easy, but overcoming them is one of the key purposes of living. From this perspective, negative emotions actually make our lives meaningful.

Negative emotions are difficult to overcome, because they reflect the presence of a 'negative mental capital stock', which is not going to disappear overnight. The negative mental capital stock has been accumulated over a long time in the past. Given the negative capital stock, we may hate someone, we may feel jealous and we may be easily irritated. Two households living next door to each other may accumulate so much hate and anger toward each other that a minor incident could trigger a real fight. As a matter of fact I have read a true story of someone killing his neighbour in great fury because of the noise he produced.

As is sometimes pointed out, hatred is often manipulated for political purposes by artful politicians. The most well-known example in history is of course Adolf Hitler's manipulation of Germans' hatred for the Jews. Hitler blamed Germany's defeat in the First World War on the Jews, and created a common enemy to unite the German people. Coming to terms with negative emotions is recognising the potentially destructive effects of these negative emotions, and realising that there is often not a single good explanation for these emotions.

Coming to terms with negative emotions is not to suppress them, but to recognise their potential harmful effects and then attempt to let out these emotions in the least harmful or preferably even totally harmless way, and at the same time try to reason ourselves out of these emotions over the longer run.

Seligman (2002) has this to say about negative emotions: 'Expressed and dwelt upon . . . emotions multiply and imprison you in a vicious cycle of dealing fruitlessly with past wrongs.' It is a pity that a person, thus 'imprisoned', often loses control of himself, and could in some circumstances let out his emotions in horrific, destructive ways.

One example of such horrific, destructive ways of letting out one's negative emotions is the Oakland, California campus shooting in 2012. A former student gunned down and killed a total of seven people and wounded three others at an Oakland nursing college. He had held a grudge against the school for being expelled, was deeply in debt with tens of thousands of dollars in federal tax liens against him, and two of his immediate family had died the previous year. 'We've learned that the suspect was upset with the administration at the school. He was also upset that students in the past, when he attended the school, mistreated him, disrespected him, and things of that nature', Oakland Police Chief Howard

Jordan said on *Good Morning America*.² It is easy to cite dozens of tragedies involving angry people killing and hurting innocent people.

Understandably, for some people 'reasoning oneself out of the negative emotions' is very difficult, as the anger may be explosive and spontaneous. The reason why it is so difficult is that the habit of allowing negative emotions to explode has already been formed. The negative capital is there. Recognising the nature of the problem is the beginning of the solution.

Instead of recognising that the negative emotions are potentially harmful, some people have chosen to identify themselves with those emotions, and 'reason' that they are well justified to avenge their grievances, or to create chaos and call upon society to 'correct' itself.

The Norway massacre on 22 July 2011, involving a car bomb exploding in Oslo and a shooting spree shortly after on the island of Utøya, by a 32-year-old Norwegian, Anders Behring Breivik, is a classic example of terrible acts being self-justified by a self-professed worthy cause. At his trial for the killing of 77 people and injuring others, Breivik declared: 'I acknowledge the acts, but not criminal guilt, and I claim legitimate defence.' There was no trace of remorse, only self-congratulation on his success of capturing national and international attention for his cause, which was summarised in a manifesto titled '2083: A European Declaration of Independence', bearing the name 'Andrew Berwick' – the English version of his name. He was angry with the flood of Muslims into his country and into Europe and with politicians who allowed this to happen.

It is clear that Breivik had felt threatened. He saw Muslims as alien to his culture and acted to 'defend' what he believed was his entitlement – a Norway and a Europe free of Muslims. But what was the cause of the 'mental bad' associated with the immigration of Muslims to Europe? Was it just because they were different, or was it because they were associated with some undesirable behaviour? What can be done to alleviate the mental bads? Can people be educated to become more tolerant of people who are different from them? Should Muslims work harder to win others' trust and to avoid producing the negative impressions people may have of them? Rather than simply putting the blame on one person we need to understand how the mental bads 'threat' and 'anxiety' were produced.

Breivik certainly needs to be punished for his acts, regardless of how he justified his actions. But more important is that we need to know that many violent acts have their seeds in mental bads, and that their perpetrators also routinely justify their antisocial behavior just as Breivik did. Much family violence can be seen in this light. In each case innocent people are hurt, but the perpetrator may have no remorse at all, and may think that he is doing nothing wrong.

Norway, the home of Breivik, along with other Scandinavian countries, is well known for its adherence to the cause of democracy and tolerance. Yet tolerance for people who are just different implies inequality:

When a group of individuals, whether it is a group bound by a common religion or a shared ideology, boasts that they are tolerant of another group which coexists within society, they are in no way equating themselves with the tolerated group; rather, they are pronouncing themselves as superior to the tolerated group, for when we tolerate something aren't we inadvertently saying that we do not agree with it, that we do not approve of it, but nevertheless, we will let it coexist alongside of us?

This observation comes from an article on the website of the International Raoul Wallenberg Foundation, which is devoted to promoting 'the values of solidarity and civic courage, ethical cornerstones of the Saviors of the Holocaust'.[3]

So we have discovered that the root of some of the most dangerous negative emotions that haunt humankind include the failure to see the solidarity of mankind and a disrespect toward life. Coming to terms with our negative emotions requires our cultural and educational programmes to work hard to promote the values of respect for all human life. Any group, religious, political, or otherwise, that preaches the contrary, should not be tolerated in a civilised society because it is socially destructive. Such groups are subversive of the common values that bond humankind together, destroy mental goods, create mental bads and form what may be called *negative social capital*.

Conclusions

'Negative emotions' are part of life. But they are only a part of life. They could bode ill or well, depending on how we deal with them. Because of this, 'negative emotions' may not be negative at all. If we let them take over our speech and our acts, they could feed other people's negative emotions, and mutually reinforce them in the process. They 'multiply and imprison you in a vicious cycle'. They could bring catastrophic consequences. On the other hand, if we confront our negative emotions positively, their influences subside and the energy that feeds those negative emotions is transformed into positive emotions that produce positive influences. We grow stronger, and gain happiness in the understanding that we have overcome the negative emotions. Having gone through them ourselves, we gain an insight into how they may inflict damages on others and how we may cope with them. We develop a better sense of the common roots that we share.

Notes

1 scaredmonkeys.com/2010/06/11/20-people-killed-in-flash-flood-in-arkansas-as-hikers-campers-swept-away-dozens-missing/.
2 www.aljazeerah.info/News/2012/April/4%20n/Oakland%20Shooter,%20One%20Goh,%20Upset%20with%20Students%20Disrespect,%20Unfair%20Administration.htm.
3 www.raoulwallenberg.net/articles/tolerance/.

Chapter 14

The paradox of choice

More choices and more sophisticated products need not translate into greater happiness

Introduction

Psychologist Barry Schwartz's 2004 book, *The Paradox of Choice – Why More is Less*, is a blow to one of the central assumptions of traditional economics. Economists traditionally assume that more is better, and more choice is always better than less choice. This stems from a misguided understanding of rationality. The notion of rationality in economics is simply based on the observation that human behaviour typically is motivated by some purpose. To the extent that people want to achieve their purpose, but there are dilemmas involving trade-offs, people would *want* to make the choice that best furthers their purpose. This is 'maximisation' or 'optimisation'. But wanting to make the best choice does not mean that people are always *capable* of making the best choice. This is because choices must be based on perceived options and perceived payoffs from the options. But perceptions are *always* flawed. When the perceptions do not deviate too far from reality, people can still achieve a high level of utility, where utility is just another word for the intended purpose. But when the perceptions deviate from the reality significantly, or when people are confused, they are likely to fail badly in achieving their purpose.

Schwartz's book shows that when there are too many choices, people may get confused. They know that they lack the information about the payoffs from all the choices to make the best choice, and they worry about making a wrong choice and missing out on a much better choice. This worry, unfortunately, is a mental bad, which undermines the welfare of the person independently of a possible decision over an inferior choice.

Limited capacity to process information

If people have an unlimited capacity to process information, *a priori*, having more choices will always be better than having fewer choices, because there will be greater chances of coming across a better option than hitherto available. However, our lives are finite, and our capacity to process information within a short space of time is limited. Processing information requires an effort and is taxing on our scarce resources, and may or may not be worthwhile. When an employer wants to recruit staff, he would not let his advertisement run for many days, and he normally would set a deadline. Although not being able to wait much longer may be one reason for setting a deadline, the cost of having to screen many candidates may also be a reason. In an attempt to process too much information in too short a time, people may get confused. Some people may even show anxiety at being confronted with too many choices.

Having more choices does not always cause more anxiety. If the decision is over some relatively trivial matter, it is generally not a problem at all. A diner offered a lot of choices on the menu generally will not panic. He may simply pick from the meals with which he is familiar, and from time to time may try some of the other meals for the first time, and enjoy being delighted by an occasional pleasant surprise. Picking on something that 'tastes terrible' is after all not the end of the world, and is easily dismissed and will not lead to a noticeable fall in happiness.

On the other hand, some choices will prove difficult. Having the choice of a partner among several, each of whom is attractive in his or her own way, may seem a good thing, but could present difficulties. Mary is very beautiful, but so is Pauline. Marilyn may not look as attractive, but she has a very pleasant character, and has a very nice and gentle voice, and she gives me support and encouragement each time I am down. But I really do enjoy being with Mary, and Pauline has that sense of humour and is always well organised, and loves music, which I love too. Consider the dilemma that a young man or a young woman faces looking for a soul mate, and it is not difficult to see that having multiple choices could be very difficult for some people.

This difficulty in part has to do with the fact that the choices in real life involve trade-offs, and also with the fact that, especially in personal relationships, emotions are involved. When in the end you have to choose among several possible mates, having to sever previous relationships may be emotionally very difficult. The fact that most major choices in our lives are discrete – you may choose *A* or *B* or *C*, but never some of each – may make people confused. Some people simply cannot make up their minds. This is further complicated by the fact that the future is uncertain. In a sense every choice is a gamble.

One online poll turned in the results shown in Figure 14.1[1]: from this poll, as much as 20 per cent of those polled claimed that they had thought they had married their soul mates, but that they were wrong. The poll suggests that not many marriages are 'successful'. It will be helpful to find out why so many marriages are unsuccessful. Is it because people simply placed the wrong bet?

Actually, choosing a mate is not entirely a gamble. My analysis of the relationship between marriage and happiness led me to conclude that successful marriages require an abundance of mental capital. Choosing a mate with strong mental capital – someone who has a loving personality, who has a good sense of proportion and who has a habit of reflecting and learning, who is prepared to face adversity and does not shy away from difficulties, and who has a clear purpose in life and actively pursues his/her goals – is far more important than choosing someone with good looks.

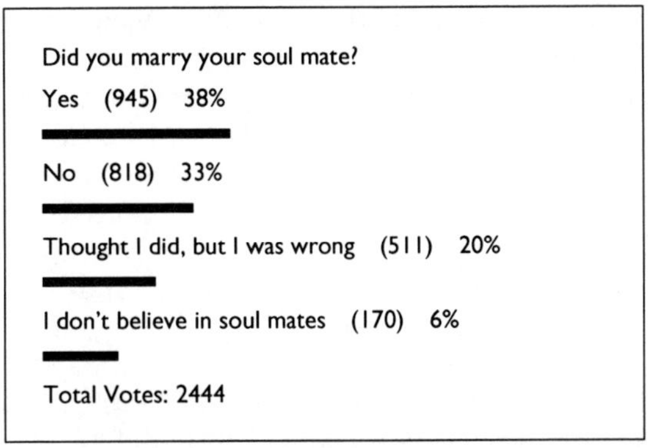

```
Did you marry your soul mate?
Yes   (945)   38%
▬▬▬▬▬▬▬
No    (818)   33%
▬▬▬▬▬▬
Thought I did, but I was wrong   (511)   20%
▬▬▬▬
I don't believe in soul mates   (170)   6%
▬▬
Total Votes: 2444
```

Figure 14.1 Results of an online marriage happiness poll.

Thus when confronted with many choices, instead of being confused by them, recognising the few key criteria for making the choice and sticking to them will allow us to make decisions that benefit us over the longer run. With the key criteria determined, it will be much easier to discard all the irrelevant choices, so you can focus on the few 'short-listed' candidates and make your final choice.

Simple is beautiful

In the 1970s, Schumacher wrote a very influential book, *Small is Beautiful* (1973). Schumacher was a respected economist who had served as the Chief Economic Advisor to the UK National Coal Board. His thesis is related to our subject in this chapter. He believes that enough is enough, and asks us to be contented with a simple life and to think more about sustainable development than about economic growth *per se*. He argues that 'the aim of human endeavour' ought to be 'to obtain the maximum amount of wellbeing with the minimum amount of consumption, since consumption is merely a means to human well-being'.

> Thus, if the purpose of clothing is a certain amount of temperature comfort and an attractive appearance, the task is to attain this purpose with the smallest possible effort, that is, with the smallest annual destruction of cloth and with the help of designs that involve the smallest possible input of toil. The less toil there is, the more time and strength is left for artistic creativity.

He goes on to argue for local production to fill local needs, as 'dependence on imports from afar and the consequent need to produce for export to unknown and distant peoples is highly uneconomic and justifiable only in exceptional cases and on a small scale'.

This appears indeed alien to a basic tenet in economics: free trade and free markets work like an invisible hand to further the common good. Adam Smith (1759) taught that division of labour is limited by the extent of the market. With globalisation, the extent of the market has grown to a size never known before, and the production of goods has never been as 'fragmented' as it is today. All this has given rise to a counter-movement, and author and filmmaker Helena Norberg-Hodge took up the mission first raised by Schumacher: a return to the *localisation* of production using local resources, rather than the relentless expansion of world trade, and a renewed emphasis on simplicity, ecological awareness and the spirit of the local community. Helena Norberg-Hodge rightly noted that the attainment of happiness has much to do with culture, and she founded the International Society for Ecology and Culture, and made two films, each of which was translated to over 50 languages: *Ancient Futures* (1991) and *The Economics of Happiness* (2011).

Notwithstanding the effort of many people joining hands to fight globalisation, globalisation as a phenomenon is likely to continue. But the key message of all these activists is really for us not to confuse means with ends. After all, life is for us to enjoy, and simplicity is beautiful. A good understanding of what we really want will help us avoid *excessive globalisation*, *excessive sophistication* and *excessive division of labour*. Economics tells us there is often too much of a good thing. Excessive globalisation happens when local cultures are drowned out by the dominant cultures that dominate because they are driven by huge financial incentives. Excessive sophistication happens when the sophistication no longer serves us. Excessive division of labour happens when workers lose a sense of purpose. When globalisation is creating mental bads, such as a sense of loss and anxiety that more than offset all the good that it brings about, globalisation will have become excessive. A world without excesses is a simpler, more beautiful world.

Conclusions

Our capacity to make informed choices is limited. However, we normally will preserve this capacity by simply ignoring some of the available choices, on the assumption that the cost of processing the information about them is higher than the expected benefit of a better choice. Moreover, when the consequence of a choice is relatively minor we may not even bother to study the choices at all. In picking from a menu, many of us simply make more or less the same choice each time, venturing to the unfamiliar only occasionally. The 'paradox of choice' in these cases will not occur.

However, there are times when we have to make a choice between several options that are attractive in their own ways and that may make a big difference in our lives. Here the paradox of choice will surface. Making a choice between two very attractive job offers may be difficult. Making a choice between ten very attractive job offers with different career paths could give you many sleepless nights.

Making a choice between two very attractive prospects for a marriage is difficult. Making a choice between three very attractive prospects could be even more so.

The fact is that sometimes we really do not know which will turn out better. After discarding those that are not so attractive, telling which one on the short list is the best choice may be just impossible. We need to understand that we will never know, and we need to understand that in life there is always uncertainty. We will make the choice anyway. And after you have made your difficult choice, you should not look back, since looking back is not going to help at all. After making the choice, you will have to do the best to make your choice work out.

Often, making the choice may not really be that difficult 'if we know what we want'. Here what we want refers to our values and priorities. Of course it is up to each person to decide his own values and priorities, and it is not for anyone else to tell him what they should be. The purpose of this chapter is to suggest only that human beings are subject to distractions. Here again mindfulness can make a big difference. The mindful person is not easily distracted and will pick what he wants. When we say simple is beautiful, it is only because most of our needs are really simple. When we know our needs and dismiss the distractions, life becomes that much simpler and that much more enjoyable.

Note

1 marriage.about.com/gi/pages/poll.htm?linkback=http://marriage.about.com/od/soulmates/qt/pollsoulmates.htm&poll_id=0166744265 accessed April 26, 2012.

Chapter 15

The holistic perspective on life, successful living and happiness

Introduction

John Maynard Keynes said in the long run we are all dead. His central message however is not one of pessimism. Rather, it is very positive. It reminds us that we cannot wait: we need to do what we can when we are alive, since we can do nothing after we have died. His reminder gives imperative to the economics of life.

Economics is both an art and a science. The substance of this book is, though, mainly about economics as an art and not so much about economics as a science. Economics as an art is about how we may make better decisions. Economics as a science is the study of how people actually make decisions in their lives. The former subject is mainly practical; the latter subject is mainly intellectual. The art, nevertheless, has to be grounded on what we know about human nature scientifically, and that requires taking what we are as a fact and a constraint.

Behavioural economists tell us that human beings often do not act rationally. By this they mean that their choices often defeat their own purpose. The basic tenet of 'revealed preference', namely 'to choose is to prefer', is both wrong and misleading. In real life, choices are inevitable, and often times people are not sure if they prefer what they choose. They may be misled by their flawed perceptions; they may follow others' behaviour instinctively; they may be unable to control themselves and fall prey to their impulsive behaviour; they may be limited by the inadequacy of their mental capital. For whichever reason they fail in making the right choices, they will not live happily.

Successful living is about making intelligent choices through life, so that we can make the most of our lives. Successful living is living a happy, fulfilling life through realising the potential for happiness that lies within each of us.

Personal development and successful living

Successful living is really about personal development or 'whole-person development', which is a somewhat overused term often found in university missions. To say that it is overused is not to say that whole personal development should not be central to university missions. The term is overused because universities may be saying this so often that they might not really think seriously about what this means, ending up merely paying lip service to whole-person development.

Personal development is about bringing out the potential that lies within, and is generally accompanied by an accumulation of positive mental capital and decumulation of negative mental capital. It is also about ridding us of our obsessions, and getting to know how we can best procure our mental goods. It is instructive to observe that blaming people for their lack of morals loses the perspective that they know no better. Actually greedy people may be merely trying to satisfy their mental good needs, such as self-esteem and sense of security, but a lack of mental capital drives them to an endless pursuit of material goods.[1] As mental capital grows, happiness grows. What used to bother you suddenly bothers you no more, while what used to elude your attention suddenly is rediscovered and becomes a source of delight.

Some may argue that success should be defined by the individual, so imposing one interpretation of successful living as the correct one and as personal development would be illiberal. But personal development as realising one's potential is very broad and very liberal. People have different strengths and weaknesses and it is up to them to develop their potential in their unique ways. The bottom line is that we are all human beings, and that we all as human beings have to do the best with our life, and learning to do the best with our life is personal development. Each person can choose his own career; each person has to decide for himself what is important and what is not; and each person has to choose his own lifestyle. Personal development is entirely personal, and even though in the end only those who become less egoistic and who open up and embrace the world will be happy, each of us will have to discover this on his own.

Scientifically, we have evidence that people who love more, people who have a sense of proportion and self-control and who see success more as doing the best they can than in terms of doing better than others, people who can 'tough it out' no matter what, and people who live an active life with a clear purpose will be happy. If someone deviates from this 'happiness formula' of Love, Insight, Fortitude and Engagement, and still discovers happiness, he would be a rare exception, because my analysis is based on a huge sample and across different cultures. Ultimately we have to be honest with ourselves, and reflect on what we do and how we see things and if what we do and how we see things make us happy. Personal development requires that honesty with ourselves.

Daily happiness versus enduring happiness

As we accumulate more mental capital, we respond to different situations in naturally wise ways. Instead of frowning or panicking over an adverse situation, we capitalise on what assets we still have to deal with that situation in the best manner. We are able to cope with pressures and frustrations and losses better. We do not care so much about whether things have turned out the way we would like. We face each day with a passion: to enjoy it if it is enjoyable, to learn from it if there is a lesson to be learnt, to test our strength and to train to be stronger if the day is rough and tough. We do not worry so much about whether an experience or an activity is enjoyable, boring, hard or a struggle. Daily or hourly happiness gradually will not count so much, as we have our eyes on a broader and farther landscape. In this way, we gradually acquire an attitude that fosters enduring happiness, and rejoice in discovering that we actually gain something each day, no matter what.

This is why I have some problems with the 'National Time Accounting' (NTA) work pioneered by Alan B. Krueger, Daniel Kahneman, David Schkade, Norbert Schwarz, Arthur A. Stone (KKSSS).[2] They have described their approach thus:

> Our project is distinguished from past efforts in that we approach NTA from more of a psychological well-being and Experience Sampling Method (ESM) perspective. For example, our measure of emotional experience is multi-dimensional, reflecting different core affective dimensions. And like ESM, we try to measure the feelings that were experienced during different uses of time as closely as possible. We also developed an easily interpretable and defensible metric of subjective well-being, which combines the data on affective experience and time use to measure the proportion of time spent in an unpleasant state.

They cited the work of Dow and Juster (1985) and Juster *et al.* (1985), who emphasised the notion of 'process benefits', or the flow of utility that accrues during particular activities, such as work and consumption. With the assumption that process benefits from activities are separable, utility can be written as:

Total utility = Utility from work + Utility from cooking + Utility from eating

Utility from work is dependent on the time spent on work and the amount of clothing; utility from cooking is dependent on the time spent on cooking, the amount of clothing and the quantity of food; utility from eating is dependent on the time spent eating, the amount of clothing and amount of meals cooked. This notion of process benefits is related to the concept of experienced utility proposed by Kahneman. KKSSS:

> define an individual's experienced happiness on a given day by the average value of this dimension of affective experience for that day. Experienced happiness, so defined, is influenced by the individual's allocation of time: a longer lunch and a shorter commute make for a better day.

In a recent paper (Ho, 2011b) I noted that the amount of enjoyment or displeasure from an activity was often not intrinsic to that activity. Often it depends on the individual's state of mind. Cooking can be fun, or it can be a chore. Attending a concert can be very pleasurable, but it could also be a pain, if a person while attending the concert keeps thinking about the work that he has yet to do, or the grudge that he has against someone who had treated him unfairly. I proposed that happiness may comprise three components, and they may not be additive. These are 'prospective happiness', 'process happiness' and 'retrospective happiness'. Prospective happiness refers to the happiness or unhappiness that one experiences as one faces a welcomed or feared prospect. We can be very happy looking forward to a wedding, or a new job, or meeting someone we have missed for many years. We can be very unhappy regretting something that we had done before, or very happy cherishing the sweet moments that we had in the past spending time with our beloved. Such prospective and retrospective emotions will affect the enjoyment from an ongoing activity.

Then there is the consideration that many mental goods depend on unpleasant activities, and the enjoyment of mental goods will not be reflected in the time accounting surveys, because these surveys would only relate feelings of happiness or unhappiness to specific activities. Without the arduous training, there can be no sense of achievement for an athlete who wins in a game. What is more, without going through pain and suffering, it will be impossible to understand other people's pain and suffering, and there can be no empathy, no love and no appreciation.

Actually, in a chapter written by David Cutler and collected in the KKSSS volume, these points are recognised. 'Pleasures of wealth, skill, amity, a good name, piety, and benevolence are generally missing' from the U-index. KKSSS would not dismiss these criticisms, but noted that NTA still offers a dimension of wellbeing that is not captured in conventional economic statistics.

Holistic living

So personal development is a process of gradually accepting life as it is, in its entirety, and unleashing the potential within us. The interesting thing is that we do not really need to wait till we have finally unleashed all the potential within us to become happy. The process itself is most fulfilling. This comes from personal experience as well as the observation that many people who honestly and earnestly embrace personal development as a life goal suddenly become much more cheerful. Seeing ourselves gradually overcoming barriers, both physical and mental, is fulfilling. Like a chick breaking the egg shell breathing the first breath of air from the outside, the joy is immense. I have seen many handicapped people – blind people, deaf people, people who have lost limbs, people who have lost their speech – find fulfilment in their lives. I have seen people who have shown a sea change in their outlook having recovered from a near-death experience and then start treasuring the days that are left and finding meaning in their lives.

This readily brings to mind the blogger's scepticism over Ototake (see Chapter 9): 'Are we to believe in all his twenty-five years he has never had even one dark night of the soul—wondering, 'Why me? . . . if Oto is completely happy, then he is either one in a million, or he is a saint.' We agree that the severe handicaps faced by Ototake and others certainly are sources of tremendous hardship and suffering. The fact that Ototake finds his life fulfilling and is 'perfectly happy' does not mean the handicap did not matter. This is exactly why 'perfectly happy' is not the same as 'perfectly satisfied'. It would be nice if the handicaps could be removed, so the blind could see and the deaf could hear again, and the limbless could walk and could handle things. It is also true that some people really live miserably because of these handicaps. But from a holistic viewpoint, all the suffering that humanity has endured allows us to know love, empathy, support, courage, endurance and kindness. It is of no use complaining at all. If someone is already handicapped, that means he should work harder to put into good use what functionality he still has. While Ototake in the east would not be handicapped by his apparent handicaps, the handicaps with which he is born have, in a sense, become an asset to him as he preaches his message of engaged and courageous living. Adrian Anantawan in the west, in the United States, is yet another example of fruitful, courageous and earnest living. He is a world-class violinist, but unbelievably, he was born without a right hand! With loving parents who wanted to give their 9-year-old child a musical instrument despite his handicap, and thanks to inventive engineers, the young boy was finally given a custom-made prosthetic to hold the bow. This device, made out of plaster, aluminium and Velcro straps, has since allowed Adrian to play and to achieve world-class status.

The following excerpt of what he had to say from an interview with a CNN reporter is truly remarkable and instructive:

> In most of these stories [of people using various ingenious ways to overcome handicaps], it's never about the technique or technology that is important, but the desire to live life authentically and creatively. We often forget even 'traditional' musical instruments are technological adaptations in their own right—they are tools to manipulate sound in a way that we couldn't do with our bodies alone.[3]

To be able to grow up despite everything gives us a great sense of accomplishment, and a great sense of joy. Think about the trophy that an athlete wins because he really trains hard and does his very best. Would a trophy mean much if it was within easy reach, and if not much effort were needed?

Holistic living is looking beyond our handicaps, and looking beyond the pain or the joy of the moment. Our lives will be much more meaningful and our potential will be more likely to be realised when life is viewed in its entirety. With a broader view and a longer view, giving up will be out of the question. We must never allow ourselves to lose the war, though we may lose a battle. The 'war' is the war against our own fears, our anxiety, our narrow-mindedness and our shortcomings in the mind, which is often the single truly inhibiting factor. The mind is often what prevents us from capitalising on the strengths that we have.

Spiritual living

The goal of all personal development is 'spiritual living'. Spiritual living, however, is nothing mystical. Nor does it mean anything 'otherworldly'. Spiritual living is simply deep respect for life, and a life with the realisation that every human being is equally of value. The spiritual person has given up egotism, and with this has developed the ability to be passionate but not attached. Since he does not distinguish between himself and others, he will never hurt others in order to advance himself. Although he is passionate about life, and goes about his day-to-day affairs not much differently from others, he is not too attached to material things or personal relationships. His mind is free, so that he is always at ease, and able to make judgement without being biased by prejudices. He has gradually overcome his weaknesses.

Spiritual living is not beyond the ability of most people. Rather it is entirely within the ability of every person. We do not have to 'become enlightened'. All that is required is a genuine respect for life and a deep humility. With humility, it is possible to make progress on the spiritual front, and only then can we make the best use of our time, because such progress allows us truly to enjoy life. In contrast, any material gains at best will give you a momentary sense of ecstasy. This is *not* to say that material gains are of no use. The spiritual person will simply take things easy. He will not overly indulge himself, and he will neither be overjoyed with material gains nor saddened by material losses.

It does not matter if inertia makes our progress a bit slow at first. But it is important to make an honest and earnest start. Spiritual living is about living humbly and honestly. It is useful to start by making some promises to oneself:

- I promise that I shall respect life and start doing so by treasuring my own life and never harming anybody.
- I promise to do my best to make full use of the potential that life has given me.
- I promise to exercise prudence in everything I do.
- I promise to abstain from harmful substances.
- I promise not to be bogged down by obsessions of any kind.
- I promise to reflect honestly.

Traditional economics shies away from values and culture or takes them as given. As David Throsby (2001) observed:

> The fact that economic agents live, breathe, and make decisions within a cultural environment is easily observable. So, too, is the fact that this environment has some influence on shaping their preferences and regulating their behaviour . . . Yet in its formal analytics, mainstream economics has tended to disregard these influences, treating human behaviour as a manifestation of universal characteristics which can be fully captured within the individualistic, rational-choice, utility maximizing model, and seeing market equilibria as being relevant to all circumstances regardless of the historical, social or cultural context (p. 11).

But, as we have argued, culture really determines the technology of consumption, and in particular the efficiency of the household production function in generating the mental goods that people need as human beings. A spiritual life helps generate strong self-esteem, inner peace and a sense of achievement without excessively depleting our scarce resources. This is achieved because the individual can seek value and dignity in self-affirmation: there is no need to have others approve, affirm or recognise our status or value. We free ourselves from the treadmill.

From individual to society to the world

Although this book was intended as an aid to individuals as they go about their life journey, we should spend a moment looking around ourselves and pondering over what we can do in our world of conflict. Through human history, regrettably, religious conflicts have left a horrifying number of casualties and broken families, and they have not stopped. Religious conflicts historically have probably been even worse than tribal conflicts. Ironically, all religions preach peace and ask their followers not to kill. This suggests that in practice religiosity and spirituality could be quite different. But it is spirituality, not religiosity, that really promotes happiness. The spirituality of a country cannot be determined by how many temples, churches or mosques it has. Rather, spiritual capital refers to:

> the interconnectedness of the human existence that awakens each individual to the common roots of humanity. It consists of a deep respect for life that is entrenched in the institutions of the country and in the minds of the people. Interestingly, when social spiritual capital is high, individuals are much more likely to be spiritually inclined. The spiritually awakened person will then begin to transcend the kind of maximizing behavior that economists talk about.
>
> (Ho, 2011, p. 47)

In order to promote spiritual capital, the following Charter for Inter-Religious Understanding and Spiritual Development (CIRUSD) has been proposed at the end of a conference held at Lingnan University back in 2007.[4]

- All religions shall take as their mission the promotion of peace, including inner peace and peace between nations, races, and different cultures.
- All religious leaders shall accept that the different theologies of the different religions owe their origins to their different historical and cultural backgrounds. Such different theologies do not affect the commonality of their teachings in terms of spiritual practice.
- Spiritual practice requires an abstention from killing and other violent acts and a respect for life.
- Religions offer different routes to the same destination, which may be considered as adaptations to suit different peoples in different cultures.
- Substance is important, not labels. Regardless of the label, all religious practices that liberate the mind from the enslavement of greed, lust, anger, hatred, ill will, and unforgivingness are true and laudable spiritual practices.

- Spiritual practice constitutes the essential teachings of all religions, not theology. The theologies of religions may differ, and may conflict with science as we know it today, but theologies are like the parables that Jesus and the Buddha used to guide people to spiritual practice. It is the spiritual messages behind the parables that really matter, not the literal meanings.

Conclusions

This last point is really important to the economics of love, life and happiness, because the treadmill is very inefficient. If economists are interested in efficiency, it is strange that they appear to be so indifferent to this inefficiency. The only reason why they have ignored this inefficiency for so long is that they have failed to see the human need for mental goods. Even Gary Becker, widely recognised as a giant in modern economics, in the paper written with Murphy (1988) on 'rational addiction', recognised only the utility derived from consuming the addictive substance, and totally ignored the disutility from the 'mental bad' in the form of a sense of being 'hooked', i.e. losing the sense of autonomy, which is much valued by almost every human being; they also ignored the disutility associated with social disapproval or stigma due to substance abuse, which a World Health Organization study confirmed to be at or near the top among various disabilities (Newcomb *et al.*, 1993).

One nice thing about spiritual living is that it is a non-rival personal 'good'. Economists distinguish between private goods and public goods. Private goods are 'rival' in the sense that, when it is taken up and consumed by someone, it is no longer available. Others can buy what is still available in the market, but with more people buying the price goes up and what is available is effectively rationed off to people through 'price rationing'. That is, those who do not want to pay the going market price will go without it. Public goods are 'non-rival' in the sense that one's consumption does not reduce the good's availability to others. Spiritual living is *more* than an ordinary public good. It is not only non-rival, but it also produces 'external economies' on others. As one adopts spiritual living, one spreads the message of Love and Insight and Fortitude and Engagement. A culture of respect for life develops and spreads, as more and more people become spiritual.

Notes

1 The distinction between needs and wants is generally considered to be moralistic, but immoral people do what they do largely because of a failure to build up mental capital and a resulting failure to meet mental good needs.
2 See: NBER Working Paper (2009) *National Time Accounting: The Currency of Life*, downloadable from: www.nber.org/chapters/c5053.pdf.
3 See report by Brandon Griggs in CNN, updated March 22, 2013: edition.cnn.com/2013/03/15/tech/innovation/adrian-anantawan-violinist/index.html?iid=article_sidebar
4 The conference title was 'Spirituality, Value, and Culture,' and it was held on 22 June 2007 at Lingnan University in Hong Kong.

Chapter 16

Epilogue

Positive pyschology

Although positive psychology has become increasingly popular I have noticed an increase in the number of sceptics. I have read at least a couple of articles in local newspapers in Hong Kong that equate positive psychology with a cult, trying to convince people that things are better than they really are. But positive psychology cannot be positive if it is escapist or if it ignores the challenges posed by the reality that life is often hard.

Christopher Peterson has this to say about positive psychology:

> Positive psychology is the scientific study of what makes life most worth living. It is a call for psychological science and practice to be as concerned with strength as with weakness; as interested in building the best things in life as in repairing the worst; and as concerned with making the lives of normal people fulfilling as with healing pathology.[1]

As an economist I see positive psychology as 'constrained maximisation': taking the real constraints for what they are and doing the best one can, maximising one's long-term interest. This is 'positive living'. This usually would mean overcoming imagined or temporary constraints, not worrying about things beyond one's control, and not being bogged down by sunk costs and foregone losses. Positive psychology is not about dismissing the real constraints. Positive psychology is about the will to do one's very best and to achieve one's very best, given the real constraints.

Unfortunately, in real life too many people fail to achieve the happiness that lies within their reach, often because somehow they manage to make things worse than they really are. In crying over spilled milk instead of making the most out of what is still available, they are like students who could have got 80 points but through panic ended up getting only 60 points. Being positive is facing the fact that what is lost is lost, and exactly because we recognise the loss that has already been incurred, we need to treasure what is still available to us even more. Suppose someone lost $2,000 to a pickpocket. Having reported the theft to the police and done what he can to seek help, the best strategy is to learn to be more careful and to get on with life as usual. If someone keeps thinking over the loss he would be piling a 'mental good loss' *on top of* the loss of the $2,000.

Positive psychology will not accept that happiness is genetically determined. The evidence is that cases abound showing that when attitudes change, people's lives can change. Without dismissing the role of genes – a real constraint – the more important message is that the 'set range' of happiness most importantly reflects a person's mental capital, and mental capital can be accumulated over time. For many unhappy people, a decision to acquire mental capital is what it takes to start life afresh.

Categorical imperative

Professor Yew-Kwang Ng strongly detests the idea of a categorical imperative in the form of performing one's call of duty, as Kant implores. Like Professor Ng, I also believe that a 'duty' that has no bearing on happiness does not make sense and cannot be worthy of being a categorical imperative. So the difference between him and me is only apparent. From what I have learnt through years of observation, people are happiest being themselves, i.e. when they follow their hearts and do what they believe in while forgetting themselves. Following their hearts means being truthful to themselves. To me this is the highest call of duty. Thus the duty of an infant is not to worry about anything – in particular not to worry about his total dependence on others for survival, which an adult in such a situation most probably would. The infant's duty is to eat when he wants to, to urinate when he wants to and to sleep when he wants to. He does not have to think of all this as a duty. Yet that is the infant's categorical imperative. This perspective extends to adults. Following one's heart – being truthful to oneself, ready to reflect honestly, ready to learn to do better – is both the highest call of duty and the happiest thing to do.

Wouldn't that make people selfish? Again, from years of observation, people who are truthful to themselves will eventually learn that being selfish will not make them happy, and so they will learn to become more and more unselfish. Someone who tries to maximise his interest even at the expense of others' interest will only find a miserable life.

The LIFE formula

I have named Love, Insight, Fortitude and Engagement the formula to happiness. I have found, through statistical test after statistical test, that self-reported happiness is highly correlated with these qualities. Yet in truth one would only need Love and Insight, otherwise called compassion and wisdom or loving others as much as ourselves and loving God. This is taught by ancient spiritual teachers, including the Buddha and Jesus. Because Jesus is regarded as a prophet in Islam this is also the lesson for Muslims. Insight or wisdom is respecting the laws of nature, both the laws that govern the physical world and the 'laws of life'[2] that govern our mental functions and mental states. Love without understanding the laws of nature will not give us much mileage. With Love and understanding, Fortitude and Engagement come automatically. During the darkest moments in life, it is Love and wisdom that enable us to tough it out. With Love and understanding, it will be silly not to live each day positively and actively. This is why factor analysis will not neatly distinguish between questions pertaining to Insight and Fortitude, for example. Indeed they are related. Referring to LIFE as the formula for happiness is essentially for educational purposes, only a gentle reminder that after all life is really the most important and the most valuable resource that each of us has. So treasure it and do the best with it while you can.

In separate studies in 2011 and 2012 I have tested the LIFE formula with school children aged 8–16 and with employees, and have found confirmation that it has strong predictive power for both the happiness of children and happiness of employees (happiness at work).[3] The children study shows, however, that they tend to become less loving, less wise and less happy as they grow into their teens. This appears to be associated with the rising pressures that come with adolescence. Adolescence is a big challenge both for children and for their parents. In line with earlier findings, we find that the relationship between the parents is a key driver for the love score of children and thus a key factor in explaining their happiness. The happiness at work study defines 'corporate Love', 'corporate Insight', 'corporate Fortitude' and 'corporate Engagement' and statistical analysis using a survey covering a total of 1,328 workers from over 600 firms shows that workers who find that their company is caring (corporate Love), generally reasonable and able to strike a good balance between centralisation and decentralisation (corporate Insight), able to command the will of staff to work together to meet challenges (corporate Fortitude) and able to engage workers in purposive tasks (corporate Engagement) are happier, and their companies also happen to be better performers.

Spirituality and religion

Many studies have shown that happiness is positively related to religiosity. But what is it in religiosity that makes people happy? My research shows that it is mainly the teachings of religions about spirituality, although the fellowship with members of the same faith also plays a part. But spirituality is not the monopoly of any particular religion, and people not affiliated with any religion can also be spiritual. Spiritual living, as discussed earlier, is simply living with a deep respect for life, and living with the realisation that every human being is equally of value. Spirituality however is not just humanism, and does require a degree of transcendence beyond just humanism, particularly transcendence from self-centredness. Having given up egotism, a spiritual person sees little distinction between himself and others, so he will never hurt others in order to advance himself. His mind is free, so that he is always at ease, and able to make judgement without being biased by prejudices. The more spiritual the man, the more he has overcome his weaknesses and perfected his life.

Notes

1 See: Christopher Peterson's (2008) 'What Is Positive Psychology, and What Is It Not?' *Psychology Today*, May 16. Downloadable from: www.psychologytoday.com/blog/the-good-life/200805/what-is-positive-psychology-and-what-is-it-not.
2 See John Marks Templeton's (1998) *Worldwide Laws Of Life: 200 Eternal Spiritual Principles*, Templeton Press.
3 The study on happiness of children was commissioned by the Early Childhood Development Research Foundation and funded by Henderson Land Group. The study on happiness at work was commissioned by the HK Productivity Council.

References

Achor, Shawn (2010) *The Happiness Advantage: The Seven Principles of Positive Psychology That Fuel Success and Performance at Work*, Crown Business.
Achor, Shawn (2012) "Is Happiness the Secret of Success?" March 19, CNN. Downloadable from: edition.cnn.com/2012/03/19/opinion/happiness-success-achor/index.html?hpt=hp_c2.
Ariely, Dan (2008) *Predictably Irrational: The Hidden Forces That Shape Our Decisions*, HarperCollins.
Banerjee, A. and E. Duflo (2012) *Poor Economics*, Penguin Books.
Becker, Gary (1965) "A Theory of Allocation of Time," *Economic Journal*, 75(299): 493–517.
Becker, Gary (1998) *The Economics of Life: From Baseball to Affirmative Action to Immigration, How Real-World Issues Affect Our Everyday Life*, McGraw Hill.
Becker, G. S. and K. M. Murphy (1988) "A Theory of Rational Addiction," *Journal of Political Economy*, 96: 675–700.
Benabou, Roland and Jean Tirole (2003) "Intrinsic and Extrinsic Motivation," *Review of Economic Studies*, 70: 489–520.
Blanchflower, David G. and Andrew Oswald (2007) "Is Well-Being U-shaped over the Life Cycle?" National Bureau of Economic Research Working Paper 12935. Downloadable from: www.nber.org/papers/w12935
Bradberry, Travis and Jean Greaves (2009) *Emotional Intelligence 2.0*, TalentSmart.
Brickman, Phillip, Dan Coates and Ronnie Janoff-Bulman (1978) "Lottery Winners and Accident Victims: Is Happiness Relative?" *Journal of Personality and Social Psychology*, 36: 917–927.
Claiborn, James and Cherry Pedrick (2001) *The Habit Change Workbook: How to Break Bad Habits and Form Good Ones*, New Harbinger Publications
Cookerly, John R. (2001) *Recovering Love: Codependency to CoRecovery*, IUniverse.
Dana Alliance for Brain Initiatives and the NRTA (2009): *Successful Aging and Your Brain*. Downloadable from: www.dana.org/uploadedFiles/The_Dana_Alliances/Staying_Sharp/Successful%20Aging%20and%20Your%20Brain.pdf.
De Bono, Edward (1970). *Lateral Thinking: Creativity Step by Step*, Harper & Row.
Deci, E. (1975) *Intrinsic Motivation*, Plenum Press.
de Graaf, John, David Wann and Thomas H. Naylor (2002) *Affluenza: The All-Consuming Epidemic*, Berrett-Koehler Publishers.
Deng, Xin and Yew-Kwang Ng (2004) "Optimal Taxation on Mixed Diamond Goods: Implications for Private Car Ownership in China," *Pacific Economic Review*, 9 (4): 293–306.

References

Diener, Ed and Robert Biswas-Diener (2011) *Unlocking the Mysteries of Psychological Wealth*, John Wiley.

Dow, Gregory K. and F. Thomas Juster (1985) "Goods, Time, and Well-being: The Joint Dependence Problem," in F. Thomas Juster and Frank P. Stafford (eds.), *Time, Goods, and Well-Being*, Survey Research Center, Institute for Social Research, University of Michigan, Ann Arbor, pp. 397–413.

Duhigg, Charles (2012) *The Power of Habit: Why We Do What We Do in Life and Business*, Random House.

Easterlin, Richard A. (1974) "Does Economic Growth Improve the Human Lot?" in Paul A. David and Melvin W. Reder (eds.), *Nations and Households in Economic Growth: Essays in Honor of Moses Abramovitz*, Academic Press, Inc.

Easterlin, Richard A., Laura Angelescu McVey, Malgorzata Switek, Onnicha Sawangfa and Jacqueline Smith Zweig (2010) "The Happiness–income Paradox Revisited," *Proceedings of the National Academy of Sciences of the United States of America*, 107 (52): 22463–22468.

Frank, Robert (2008) *The Economic Naturalist: Why Economics Explains Almost Everything*, Basic Books.

Frijters, Paul and Tony Beatton (2012) "The Mystery of the U-shaped Relationship Between Happiness and Age," *Journal of Economic Behavior and Organization*, 82 (2–3), 525–542.

Fromm, Erich (1956) *The Art of Loving*, Harper & Row.

Galbraith, John Kenneth (1958) *The Affluent Society*, Hamish Hamilton.

Gino, Francesca and Lamar Pierce (2009) "The Abundance Effect: Unethical Behavior in the Presence of Wealth," *Organizational Behavior and Human Decision Processes*, 109: 142–155.

Harford, Tim (2005) *The Undercover Economist*, Little, Brown.

Harford, Tim (2009) *The Logic of Life: Uncovering the New Economics of Everything*, Little, Brown.

Hatfield, E., Cacioppo, J.T. and Rapson, R.L. (1993) Emotional contagion. *Current Directions in Psychological Science*, 2: 96–99.

Hicks, J.R. (1939) *Value and Capital, An Inquiry into some Fundamental Principles of Economic Theory*, Clarendon Press.

Ho, Lok Sang (2001) *Principles of Public Policy Practice*, Kluwer.

Ho, Lok Sang (2011a) *Human Spirituality and Happiness*, Authorhouse.

Ho, Lok Sang (2011b) "Hong Kong's Happiness Indices: What they Tell us About LIFE?" *Journal of Socio-Economics*, 40: 564–572.

Ho, Lok Sang (2012) *Public Policy and the Public Interest*, Routledge.

Ho, Lok Sang (2013) "Happiness of Children as they Grow into their Teens: The Hong Kong Case," *CPPS Working Paper Series*. No. 93. Downloadable from: commons.ln.edu.hk/cppswp/93.

Juster, F. T., P. Courant and G. K. Dow. (1985) "A Conceptual Framework for the Analysis of Time Allocation Data," in: F. Thomas Juster and Frank P. Stafford (eds.), *Time Goods and Well-Being*. Survey Research Center, Institute for Social Research, University of Michigan, Ann Arbor.

Kahneman, Daniel and Angus Deaton (2010) "High Income Improves Evaluation of Life but not Emotional Well-Being," *Proceedings of the National Academy of Sciences of the United States of America*, 107(38): 16489–16493. Downloadable from: www.pnas.org/content/107/38/16489.full?sid=6699db95-04ed-45af-8450-074fe609aa6f.

Kant, Immanuel (1964) *Groundwork of the Metaphysics of Morals*, translated by H. J. Paton, Harper Torchbooks.

Kasser, T. (2003) *The High Price of Materialism*, MIT Press.

Kasser, T. (2009) "Can Buddhism and Consumerism Harmonize? A Review of the Psychological Evidence," *Journal of Religion and Culture*, 2: 167–193.

Kasser, T. and R. M. Ryan (1993) "A Dark Side of the American Dream: Correlates of Financial Success as a Central Life Aspiration," *Journal of Personality and Social Psychology*, 65: 410–422.

Kasser, T. and R. M. Ryan (1996) "Further Examining the American Dream: Differential Correlates of Intrinsic and Extrinsic Goals," *Personality and Social Psychology Bulletin*, 22: 280–287.

Kasser, T. and R. M. Ryan (2001) "Be Careful What you Wish For: Optimal Functioning and the Relative Attainment of Intrinsic and Extrinsic Goals," in P. Schmuck and K. M. Sheldon (eds.), *Life Goals and Well-being: Towards a Positive Psychology of Human Striving*, Hogrefe & Huber, pp. 116–131.

Kasser, T., R. M. Ryan, C. E. Couchman, and K. M. Sheldon (2004) "Materialistic Values: Their Causes and Consequences," in T. Kasser and A.D. Kenner (eds.), *Psychology and Consumer Culture: The Struggle for a Good Life in a Materialistic World*, American Psychological Association, pp. 11–28.

Keynes, John Maynard (1923) *A Tract on Monetary Reform*, Prometheus Books, Chapter 3.

Kruegar, Alan B. (ed.) (2009) *Measuring the Subjective Well-being of Nations: National Accounts of Time-use and Well-being*, National Bureau of Economic Research.

Lancaster, Kelvin (1966) "A New Approach to Consumption Theory," *Journal of Political Economy*, 74 (2): 132–157.

Landsburg, Steven E. (2012) *The Armchair Economist: Economics and Everyday Life*, Free Press.

Levitt, Steven and Stephen J. Dubner (2005) *Freakonomics: A Rogue Economist Explores the Hidden Side of Everything*, William Morrow/HarperCollins.

Levitt, Steven and Stephen J. Dubner (2009) *Superfreakonomics: Global Cooling, Patriotic Prostitutes, and Why Suicide Bombers Should Buy Life Insurance*, HarperCollins.

Luthans F. and C. M. Youssef (2004). "Human, Social, and now Positive Psychological Capital Management: Investing in People for Competitive Advantage," *Organizational Dynamics*, 33(2): 143–160.

Maslow, Abraham (1954). *Motivation and Personality*, Harper.

Mogilner, Cassie, Sepandar D. Kamvar and Jennifer Aaker (2011) "The Shifting Meaning of Happiness," *Social Psychological and Personality Science*, 2: 395–402.

Newcomb, M. D., L. M. Scheier, and P. M. Bentler (1993). "Effects of Adolescent Drug Use on Adult Mental Health: A Prospective Study of a Community Sample," *Experimental and Clinical Psychopharmacology*, 1(1–4): 215–241.

Ng, Yew-Kwang (1987) 'Diamonds Are a Government's Best Friend: Burden-free Taxes on Goods Valued for their Values,' *American Economic Review*, 77: 186–191.

Ng, Yew-kwang and Lok Sang Ho (eds.) (2006) *Happiness and Public Policy: Theory, Case Studies, and Implications*, Palgrave-Macmillan.

Ng, Yew-Kwang and Siang Ng (2000) *The Road to Happiness*. Downloadable from: www.utilitarianism.com/prof-ng/

Oswald, Andrew and Stephen Wu (2010) "Objective Confirmation of Subjective Measures of Human Well-Being: Evidence from the U.S.A.," *Science*, 327 (5965): 576–579.

Ototake, Hirotada (2003) *No One's Perfect*, translated by Gerry Harcourt, Kodansha.
Page, Liam F. and Ross Donohue (2004), *Positive Psychological Capital: A Preliminary Exploration of the Construct*, Department of Management Working Paper 51/04, Monash University.
Pausch, Randy and Jeffrey Zaslow (2008) *The Last Lecture*, Hyperion.
Piff, Paul K., Daniel M. Stancato, Stéphane Côté, Rodolfo Mendoza-Denton and Dacher Keltner (2012) "Higher Social Class Predicts Increased Unethical Behavior," *Proceedings of the National Academy of Sciences*, 109 (11): 4086–4091.
Richard, A. and Rudnyckyj, D. (2009) "Economies of Affect," *Journal of the Royal Anthropological Society*, 15 (1): 55–77.
Room, R. J., Rehm, R. T. Trotter, II, A. Paglia,and T. B. Ustun (2001) "Cross-cultural Views on Stigma, Valuation, Parity and Societal Values Towards Disability," in Ustun, T. B Bedirhan, Jurgen T. Rehm, Robert T. Trotter, Jerome E. Bickenbach, Robin Room (eds.), *Disability and Culture: Universalism and Diversity*, & Huber, pp. 247–291.
Rubin, Zick (1970) "Measurement of Romantic Love," *Journal of Personality and Social Psychology*, 16(2): 265–273.
Russell, Bertrand (1996) *The Conquest of Happiness*, Liveright.
Sandel, Michael (2012) *What Money Can't Buy*, Farrar, Straus and Giroux.
Schmuck, P. (2001) "Intrinsic and Extrinsic Life Goal Preferences as Measured via Inventories and via Priming Methodologies: Mean Differences and Relations with Well-being," in P. Schmuck and K. M. Sheldon (eds.), *Life Goals and Well-being: Towards a Positive Psychology of Human Striving*, Hogrefe & Huber, pp. 11–28.
Schmuck, Peter, Tim Kasser and Richard M. Ryan (2000) "Intrinsic and Extrinsic Goals: Their Structure and Relationship to Well-Being in German and U.S. College Students," *Social Indicators Research* 50 (2): 225–241.
Schumacher E. F. (1973) *Small is Beautiful: Economics as if People Mattered*, Harper Perennial (2nd edn, 27 September 1989).
Schwartz, Barry (2004) *The Paradox of Choice – Why More Is Less*. Harper Perennial.
Seligman, Martin (2002) *Authentic Happiness*, Free Press
Seligman, Martin (2003) *Authentic Happiness*, Atria Books.
Skidelsky, Robert and Edward Skidelsky (2012) *How Much is Enough: Money and the Good Life*, Other Press.
Smith, Adam (1759) *The Theory of Moral Sentiments*, Clarendon Press, 1759/1976.
Stevenson, Betsey and Justin Wolfers (2009) "The Paradox of Declining Female Happiness," *American Economic Journal: Economic Policy* 1(2): 190–225.
Stone, Arthur A., Joseph E. Schwartz, Joan E. Broderick and Angus Deaton (2010) "A Snapshot of the Age Distribution of Psychological Well-being in the United States," *Proceedings of the National Academy of Science*, 107 (22): 9985–9990.
Szuchman, Paula and Jenny Anderson (2011) *Spousonomics: Using Economics to Master Love, Marriage, and Dirty Dishes*, Random House.
Templeton, John Marks (2008) *Worldwide Laws of Life: 200 Eternal Spiritual Principles*, Templeton Press.
Thaler, R. (1980) "Toward a Positive Theory of Consumer Choice," *Journal of Economic Behavior and Organization*, 1: 39–60.
Throsby, David (2001) *Economics and Culture*, Cambridge University Press.
Tversky, A. and Daniel Kahneman (1991) "Loss Aversion in Riskless Choice: A Reference Dependent Model," *Quarterly Journal of Economics*, 1039–1061.

Wallace, Mike and Paul Gates (2005) *Between You and Me: A Memoir*, Hyperion.
Warren, H. C. and L. Carmichael (1930) *Elements of Human Psychology* (revised edition),Houghton Mifflin, p. 333.
Wike, Victoria S. (1994) *Kant on Happiness in Ethics,* State University of New York Press.
Wood, Wendy and David T. Neal (2007) "A New Look at Habits and the Habit–Goal Interface," *Psychological Review*, 114(4): 843–863.
Zheng Fengxi (Cheng Feng-Hsi, 鄭豐喜) (1984) *A Boat in a Restless Ocean*,(汪洋中的一條船), 主人翁文化事業公司, 1984, 12th edn, Be Your Own Master Cultural Enterprises.

Index

acculturisation 28
addictive capital 21
adolescence 21, 20
advertising 11
affluenza virus 28
ageing xiii, 8, 9, 10, 47, 53
ageing, successful 9, 10
Allaire, P. A. 70
Anantawan, A. 114, 117
Anderson, J. 60, 125
Ariely xv, 1, 122
attachment 16, 17, 68, 69
autonomy i, 6, 13, 21, 26, 33, 39, 45, 46, 63, 68, 117

Banerjee, A. 15, 122
basic commodities 6, 11, 24
Bauer, P. 64
Becker, G. 2, 6, 11, 21, 24, 117
Bell, A. 38
Bentham, J. 89
big picture vii, 2, 3, 71, 74
Bradberry, T. 36, 122
Breivik, A. B. 103
Brickman, P. 79, 122
Buddha 78–80, 117, 119
Buddhism 43, 44, 124
Buffet, W. 28
bullycide xv
Butterfly Lovers x, 69

campus shooting, 2012 10, 102
capital as a means of production 16, 32
capital, human 32
capital, mental x, xv–xvii, 3–6, 19, 21, 31–9, 42, 43, 56–61, 68, 73, 75, 84, 89, 93, 100, 102, 106, 110–112, 117, 119

capital, spiritual x, 33, 34, 115–116
caring 10, 12, 16, 58, 96, 120
Carnegie Mellon University 76
categorical imperative xii, xiii, 34, 81, 82, 86, 119
causality 31, 56
Centre for Public Policy Studies, Lingnan University i, 46, 90, 91
Charter for Inter-Religious Understanding and Spiritual Development 116
cheating 64
Claiborn, J. 36, 122
comparative advantage 19, 60, 75
compassion 33, 43, 44
competition 23, 63
conspicuous consumption xvii, 29, 44, 62
constrained maximisation xiv, xv, 82, 105, 118
Cookerly, R. xi, 15, 16, 22, 122
Cooper, C. L. xvi, 122
cost benefit analysis 4
cost, information xiv
cost, sunk ix, x, 69, 70, 71, 96, 118
culturally shared norms 27–28
culture xvii, 9, 13, 21–31, 44, 49, 63, 75, 103, 108, 111, 115–117
Cutler, D. 89, 113

Dana Alliance for Brain Initiatives 10, 122
Daodejing xii, 44, 78, 80
Deaton, A. xiv, 30, 42, 47, 123, 125
Deci, E. L. 8
de Graf, J. 24, 122
decision utility xvi, 8, 122
decision variables 4, 43

Index

Declaration of War, movie 10
democracy 103
depression 96
diamond good 22, 29, 122
dictator game xv
distractions xi, 84, 109
division of labour 19, 59, 108
DNA exonerations 97
Donohue, R. xvii, 125
doping 63
Dow, G. K. 112, 123
Duflo, E. xv, 123
Duhigg, C. 35, 36, 123
duty/duties 34, 77, 81, 86, 100, 119

Easterlin paradox 30
Easterlin, R. xiv, 25, 30, 123
ecological footprint 13, 25, 28
economics of everyday life i, 1, 2, 23, 122, 124
economics of life xi, 1–10, 13, 23, 43, 110, 122
ego 16, 29, 34, 67, 80, 95, 111, 115, 120
egotism 115, 120
emotional contagion 20, 123
end goods 6, 23, 24, 29, 32
ends versus means 19, 44, 46, 65, 66, 82, 83, 108
engagement xii, xiii, xvii, 32, 43–57, 60, 61, 71, 81–87, 92, 111, 117, 119, 120
envy 24, 27, 67, 71, 72
errors xi, 94–98
evaluated time use 88–89
excesses 44, 65
excuses 35, 37
external economies 117
extrinsic motivations xvi, 8, 44, 122, 124, 125

Fan, S. 64
felicific calculus 89
financial stress 47, 49, 50, 61
Fogel, R. 34
forgive and forget 71, 95, 98
fortitude xii, xvii, 32, 43, 44–57, 60, 61, 70, 71, 73–80, 83, 92, 96, 111, 117, 119, 120
Frey, B. 14
Fromm, E. 20, 43, 68, 72, 123
functional health 5

Galbraith, K. 24, 123
Gandhi, M. 13
Gates, P. 96, 126
Gino, F. 27, 123
globalization 108
gluttony 67
Gospel According to St Matthew 78
gratitude 75, 96
Graybiel, A. 35, 36
Greaves, J. 36, 122
greed 12, 31, 67, 111, 116
growing up vs growing old 37
guilt 93, 103

habit i, xvii, 32–9, 45, 84, 85, 89, 100, 103, 106, 122, 123, 126
happiness formula, amendment to Seligman's 41
happiness formula, as L+I+F+E 43–55, 83, 111
happiness formula, as S+C+V 40, 42
happiness, as enduring level of happiness 40–3
happiness, as subjective well being xiv, 40–42, 93, 112
happiness, process 90–2, 112, 113
happiness, prospective 7, 90–2, 113
happiness, retrospective 7, 90–3, 113
happiness, transcendental 90–3
hard work 20, 54, 64, 73, 74, 75
health stock 5, 9, 21
Heckman, J. xiv
Helliwell, J. xiv
Hicks, J. R. 11, 123
Ho, L. S. x, xii, xiii, 5, 9, 14, 65, 83, 87, 112, 116, 123
Hong Kong 45–50, 53, 56, 57, 85, 89–93, 99, 117, 118, 123
honour 7, 27, 83, 96
honour killing xv, 7
hope xvii, 32, 35, 36, 39, 45, 73, 74, 77, 90
household production x, xvii, 6, 11–13, 23–31, 32, 116
human dynamics 79
human nature 1, 2, 24, 67, 69, 110
humility 44, 67, 75, 115

inertia 35, 66, 67, 69, 115
Innocence Project 97
insecurity 7, 26

insight ix, x, xii, xvi, xvii, 1, 21, 32, 43–57, 60, 61, 65–72, 80, 83, 92, 104, 111, 117, 119, 120
International Raoul Wallenberg Foundation 104
intimacy 16–17
intrinsic motivation 8, 44, 122
investing x, 5, 32, 95, 100, 124

Jackson, E. 74
Jesus 117, 119
John Templeton Foundation 34, 39, 121
Juster 112, 123

Kahneman, D. xiv, 14, 30, 42, 47, 59, 123, 125, 71, 93
Kant xii, xiii, 34, 81, 83, 86, 87, 119, 124, 126
karma 89
Kasser, T. 26, 31, 44, 124
Keynes, J. M. 110, 124
Kodak 70
Krueger, A. xiv, 93, 112, 124

Lancaster, K. 11, 124
Last Lecture, the 76, 125
lateral thinking 28, 122
laws of life 119, 121, 125, see also laws of nature
laws of nature 9, 73, 119
learning by doing 21, 37
learning skills 32
Leeson, N. 95
life expectancy 2, 5, 90
LIFE scores 46–8, 50, 53, 54, 56–8, 90, 92, 93
limiting losses 77–8
Lin, J. 74
living, holistic 133–4
living, positive 75–7, 118
living, purposive 83–4
living, spiritual 115–116
living, successful x, 4, 110–117
living, truthful x, 66, 78, 80, 83, 87
localization 108
love i, ix–xiii, xv–xvii, 5, 7, 9, 10–22, 26, 28, 29, 32, 42, 45–55, 56–61, 63, 68, 69, 75, 80, 83–7, 92, 93, 96, 111, 113, 114, 117, 119, 120, 122, 125
love, romantic 10, 16, 17, 58, 68, 69, 125

love, self 20–2
love, tough 20–1
loving economically 17–19
lust 67, 116
luxury goods 24, 26, 28, 29
Lykken, D. 42, 55

Manila 99
Marathon des Sables 64
marginal benefit 4, 84
marginal cost 4
marriage and happiness x, 13, 19, 21, 52, 56–61, 106, 107, 109
Maslow, A. xvi, 7, 62, 124
maximisation xiv, xv, 4, 81, 82 105, 118
mental bad xv, 5, 7, 8, 20–2, 63, 67, 71, 97, 103–105, 108, 117
mental capital ix, x, xv, xvi, xvii, 3, 4, 5, 19, 21, 31, 32–39, 42, 43, 45, 53, 56–61, 68, 73, 75, 84, 89, 93, 100, 102, 106, 110, 111, 117, 119,
mental goods i, v, ix, x, xv, xvi, 5–13, 16, 17, 20, 22, 24, 25, 26, 28–31, 33, 35, 44, 45, 60, 62, 64, 67, 68, 83, 104, 111, 113, 116, 117, 119
mindfulness ix, 36, 66, 85, 95, 100, 109
misfortunes 2, 77, 97, 101–2
MIT 35
Mogilner, C. 47, 53, 124
motivation, extrinsic xvi, 8, 44, 122, 124, 125
motivation, intrinsic xvi, 8, 44, 122, 124, 125
motivations xvi, 7–8, 15, 36, 37, 44, 64, 122, 124, 125
Mulcahy, A. 70
Murphy 27, 117, 122
Music 34, 35, 37, 64, 84

National Time Accounting 112, 117
Ng, Y.-K. xiii, xviii, 22, 29, 79, 119, 122, 124
Norway massacre, 2011 103
nouveau riche 24–25

objective function 65
obsession xi, 66, 68, 69.70, 71, 111, 115
obsessive-compulsive diisorder 66
Olympic Games 63
optimism xiv, xvii, 32, 35, 36, 39, 73
optimisation 105, also see maximisation

Oswald, A. xiv, 47, 122, 124
Ototake, H. 75, 76, 113, 114, 125

Page, L. F. xvii, 125
paradox of choice 105–9, 125
Pausch, R. 76, 125
Pedrick, C. 36, 122
perceived constraints 43
perceptions xiv, 1, 2, 9, 22, 105, 110
Philippines 99
Pierce, L. 27, 123
Piff, P. K. 2, 627, 125
Pope, A. 95
positive psychology i, xiv, xv, 40, 43, 77, 118–119, 121, 122, 124, 125
Prayer of Saint Francis of Assisi 44
prevention 9, 21
price rationing 117
pride 26, 29, 67
Princeton Affect and Time Survey (PATS) 88
procrastination 35
pseudo mental goods 67–8
psychological capital 73, 124, 125
pursuit, blind 26
Putnam, R. 34

quadriplegics 79

rat race xvii, 26
rational addiction 21, 117, 122
real constraints 6, 43, 118, 119
reflection 36–8, 43
reflective skills 32, 34, 37
reflexive responses 35, 37, 38
regret 85, 88, 89, 93–8, 113, 116
religion 34, 43, 66, 77, 104, 116, 117, 120, 124
resilience see fortitude
revealed preference 110
romantic affinity versus love x, 58, 59
Romantic Love 10, 16, 17, 58, 68, 69
Romantic Love Scale 16
Romeo and Juliet 17, 68, 69
Rubin, Z. 16, 58, 68, 125

Saint Francis of Assisi 44
Saviors of the Holocaust 104
Schkade, D. 93, 112
Schumacher, E.F. 107, 108, 125
Schwartz, B. i, 9

Schwarz, N. 35
self acceptance i, xvii, 32, 33, 35
self-defence mechanism i, 14, 16, 29, 30, 33, 45, 93, 111, 116
self-efficacy 40, 41, 42, 44, 66, 93, 102, 125
self-esteem i, 46, 62, 63, 113, 116
Seligman, M. 66
sense of achievement 41
sense of proportion ix, 40, 41, 42, 119
set point x, 66, 67
set range 89, 99
seven deadly sins 18, 28, 31, 107–9
severe acute respiratory syndrome (SARS) 7, 95
simple living 25, 125
Singapore 67
Skidelsky, R. 22, 108
sloth 9, 34, 104
Smith, A. 26
social capital 1
social modeling x, 83, 87
soft paternalism 108
Song of the Truthful Mind 19
sophistication, excessive 115–116
spillovers 47, 53, 93, 104, 112, 125
spiritual living x, xv, xvii, 4, 9, 10, 38, 46, 53, 56, 60, 61, 63, 64, 71, 74, 80, 106, 110–117, 122, 124
Stone, A. A. xv, 58, 79, 82, 96
successful living ix, x, 69, 70, 71, 96, 118
suicide 105, 125
sunk costs 112, 93
Szuchman, P. 60, 125

Taj Mahal 17–18
temperament and personality 22, 41, 55
Thaler, R 1, 71, 125
Thoman, G. R. 70
Throsby, D. 115, 125
total life satisfaction 30, 41, 92
traits 9, 41, 42, 89
Trump, D. 28

U-index 88, 89, 113
utilitarianism 89, 124
utility xiv, xv, xvi, 2, 6, 11, 17, 20, 21, 23, 29, 30, 40, 64, 65, 81, 89, 105, 112, 115, 117

value metrics 81, 82
vanity 62–4
voluntary factor 40–3

Wallace, M. 96, 97, 126
Wang Computers 70
Wasada University 75
Weehuizen, R. xvi, xvii
whole person development 110–111
work-life balance 6, 43, 83
World Value Survey 49–54, 56

worry or worrying xi, 13, 20, 30, 62, 64–6, 89, 90, 99, 100, 112, 118, 119
wrath 67, 79
Wright brothers 38
Wu, S. xiv, 124

Xerox 70

Yates, M. 96

Zheng F. 76, 77, 126